CLIMBING YOUR WAY TO THE BOTTOM™

CLIMBING YOUR WAY TO THE BOTTOM™

CHANGING THE WAY
YOU APPROACH YOUR JOB SEARCH

ROB SULLIVAN

PUBLISHING

Chicago

The following trademarks and servicemarks appear throughout the book: Adobe Desktop Publishing, Band-Aid, Harvard Graphics, Lotus, Microsoft Word, Nike, Pro A/R, QuickBooks, Reebok, Screaming Yellow Zonkers, SpectrumMaster, SpellCheck, Toys 'R' Us, WalMart, Zantac. These marks are owned by companies and individuals other than PurePlay Publishing or Rob Sullivan.

Although the author and publisher have researched sources to assure the accuracy and completeness of the information contained in this book, we assume no responsibility for errors, inaccuracies, omissions, or any other inconsistencies herein. Any slights against people or organizations are unintentional.

CLIMBING YOUR WAY TO THE BOTTOM™. Copyright © 1997 by Rob Sullivan. All rights reserved. No part of this book may be used or reproduced in any manner whatsoever without written permission except in the case of brief quotations embodied in critical articles or reviews. For information, write or call:

>Pure Play Publishing, Inc.
>2501 N. Lincoln Avenue, #167 B
>Chicago, IL 60614
>312-409-9448
>http:// www.pureplay.com/pureplay

Library of Congress Catalog Card Number: 95-92930

Publisher's Cataloging in Publication
(Prepared by Quality Books Inc.)

Sullivan, Rob (Robert Ryan)
  Climbing your way to the bottom : changing the way you approach your job search / Rob Sullivan.
   p. cm.
  Includes index.
  Preassigned LCCN: 95-92930
  ISBN 1-889587-72-9 (hard cover)
  ISBN 1-889587-73-7 (soft cover)

  1. Job hunting. 2. Vocational guidance. I. Title.

HF5181.S85 1996   650.14
                           QBI96-40202

Cover design by Pamela Serp
Cover art (original watercolor) by Joe Favre
Illustrations by Harry Wilson
Edited by Heidi Schlumpf and Lisa Orman
Back cover photograph by Mary Economidy
Layout by Jerald E. Durkin (Director, Jar Design) and Pamela Serp

Printed in the United States of America.  printed on recycled paper
(50% Total Recycled Fiber, 10% Post Consumer Waste)

*This book is dedicated to the undiscovered and underappreciated
artists and musicians of the world.
May we have the good sense to discover and appreciate these treasures
while they are still alive.*

*This tragically long list includes,
but is not limited to:*

Dave Crossland *(singer/songwriter)*
Eddie from Ohio *(acoustic/folk group)*
Stewart Harris *(singer/songwriter)*
Sons of the Never Wrong *(acoustic/folk group)*
Speidel, Goodrich, Goggin and Lille *(acoustic/folk group)*
The Vulgar Boatmen *(Indianapolis rock band)*
Harry Wilson *(artist)*

ABOUT THE AUTHOR

Rob Sullivan is living proof that the exercises described in this book are effective. After more than 80 interviews and a humbling series of rejections in the ultra-competitive advertising industry, Rob uncovered the secrets of job hunting. With this knowledge, Rob reapplied to Leo Burnett—the agency that rejected him the year before—and earned a coveted spot in the company's Client Service Training Program. At Burnett, Rob worked as an account executive on the Philip Morris/Marlboro, McDonald's, and John G. Shedd Aquarium accounts. He also gained extensive experience as an interviewer and campus recruiter.

In 1994, Rob decided to pursue one of his other lifelong dreams—to become a trader at the Chicago Board of Trade. This gave him the opportunity to use the same job hunting principles to reposition himself for a completely different career. Despite the fact that he had no formal experience, Rob earned a position with Cooper Neff & Associates—one of the premiere options trading firms in the world.

Through his own ongoing process of self-evaluation, Rob recognized an opportunity to combine his interests in marketing and finance. As a result, he is dedicating his talents to "marketing that makes a difference." Helping job hunters and career-changers is an important part of that objective. In addition, he has formed a company that combines his talents and interests with his dedication to Children's Memorial Medical Center in Chicago. The company has two primary goals:

- to enable artists, musicians, and entrepreneurs to make a living doing what they do best.

- to ensure that the needs of hospitalized children will be met well into the 21st Century.

The second objective flows naturally from the first because Rob will be donating a percentage of the profit—from both the business and the book—to the Family Support Services Department at Children's Memorial.

Rob has a BA in psychology from the College of the Holy Cross in Worcester, Massachusetts, and an MS in advertising from Northwestern University's Medill School of Journalism.

THE BASIS OF OPTIMISM IS SHEER TERROR.

—OSCAR WILDE

Table of Contents

ABOUT THE AUTHOR — ix

LETTER FROM THE AUTHOR — xvii

ABOUT THE ART — xx

PREFACE — xxix
   The Unmet Needs of the Educated

INTRODUCTION — xxxi
   How this Book is Different

PART 1: Creating a Marketing Plan for Yourself

CHAPTER 1
The Product: *Learning to sell yourself* — 5
   The paradox of preparation • Self-analysis

CHAPTER 2
The Category: *Careers and competitors* — 15
   Target analysis • Creating other opportunities •
   Your competition

CHAPTER 3
Creating Awareness — 21
   Understanding the concepts • Cover letters • Résumés •
   Writing samples • Building a network • Correspondence

PART 2: Making the Sale

CHAPTER 4
Consumer Perceptions — 67
Videotaped mock interviews • Informational interviews • Dressing appropriately

CHAPTER 5
Direct Selling: *The interview* — 73
What is an interview? • Making sense of a flawed process • Other interviewing styles • Handling inappropriate questions

CHAPTER 6
Improving Your Technique and Closing the Deal — 105
Believe in yourself • Learning from interviews • Beyond nervousness • Salary negotiation

PART 3: The Product Life Cycle

CHAPTER 7
The Growth Phase — 125
The view from the bottom • The gift of perspective • Giving back • Listen to your dreams

GREAT READING — 135

GLOSSARY — 139

INDEX — 143

A Letter from the Author:

Dear Future Executive:

My reasons for writing this book are both personal and professional. Although I have always enjoyed writing, I limited myself to an occasional song, poem, or letter. I never thought about writing a book. Like many of life's great opportunities, this book had more to do with timing than planning.

Over the past few years, I have received a steady stream of calls from people who needed help job hunting. For the most part, they had what it takes to succeed. They just didn't realize it. After spending countless hours working one-on-one with these people, the need for this book became clear. It is my effort to share with the professionals of tomorrow what I have learned from the executives of today. This is the book that would have made my own job search easier.

If you look at job hunting as a numbers game, the odds weigh heavily against you. Companies receive thousands of unsolicited résumés every year. Many also recruit at top colleges, universities, and business schools. This competition can be fierce, but it isn't always well prepared. With a focused strategic effort, a BA who demonstrates potential can compete successfully—even against people with advanced degrees and work experience. Simply put, the ability to market yourself effectively can be far more valuable than an advanced degree.

It would be a mistake to view *Climbing Your Way to the Bottom* as a one-size-fits-most, fill-in-the-blank career guide. You won't find short cuts or easy answers. Instead, you will discover strategies to market yourself effectively. You don't have to love marketing. And you don't have to make a career of it. But you do have to be good at it. Otherwise, your dream job will be just that—a dream.

Job hunting does not have to be difficult. You don't have to pretend to be someone you are not. You already have the only asset you need—potential. You might think you need full-time experience, an internship at a Fortune 500 company, or a network of executive contacts. You don't. Those fall strictly in the "nice-to-have" category.

As an early reader of this book, you also have the opportunity to make a difference in the lives of future readers. If this interests you, start now. Write down your expectations. Then, read the book slowly. Take notes. Do the exercises. When you finish, answer these questions:

- How did you apply the principles to your own job search?

- What did you find most helpful?

- What surprised you?

- What do you wish had been covered in greater detail?

In my life, I have learned that at precisely those times when life seems to get worse that you may actually be getting ready to make a leap. When you feel like you're getting nowhere—stagnating, even slipping backward—what you're actually doing is backing up to get a running start.

—*Dan Millman,*
"Sacred Journey of the Peaceful Warrior"

If you have ideas, comments, or questions please drop me a line. You can reach me at the address and e-mail listed below:

Rob Sullivan
c/o Pure Play Publishing
2501 N. Lincoln Ave., #167 B
Chicago, IL 60614

E-mail: **rsullivn@pureplay.com**

Best of luck. Let me know how it goes!

Rob

P.S. If you believe that people everywhere should be able to make a living doing what they do best—and you know a starving artist or musician who deserves recognition—please send me their name and a sample of their work. My business partners and I are creating a company dedicated to promoting the world's undiscovered talent. Too many people are spending their careers in unsatisfying jobs when they should be nurturing their creativity. Please help us find them.

Opposite:
Flying Through the Universe in a Lime-Green Hat
Harry Wilson © 1996. From the author's personal collection. Reprinted with permission.

ABOUT THE ART

On the following page is the first of three pictures which I have included—not so much for what they say about business—but for what they say about life. All three are the work of an extremely talented, yet relatively unknown artist named Harry Wilson.

Aside from the fact that this is one of my favorite pieces of art, I have included it because of the feeling it conveys. The picture, *Flying Through the Universe in a Lime-Green Hat,* captures the absolute excitement and sheer terror that coexist in almost any worthwhile journey. Job hunting is no exception. Embrace the fear. Have fun. Be challenged. Laugh at yourself. Allow yourself to make mistakes. When you really think about it, life is both wonderful and absurd. Don't take it too seriously.

Acknowledgements

Only within the last few years have I seen my "fiercely independent" nature as a weakness rather than a strength. As a result, I have only begun to recognize, accept and acknowledge the contributions others make to my life. You (the readers of this book) and I will never fully appreciate the extent to which professionals, friends, and family added insight to this project. But I assure you, we are both better for it.

The categories on the following pages are not mutually exclusive. Nor are they in any particular order. More than a few people deserve prominence in every category.

People who challenged and coached me

These people unselfishly shared their observations, constructive criticisms, insights, and time. Without them, neither the book nor I would have reached our respective stages of development.

- George Badecker, *improv instructor, Players' Workshop*
- Marc Blumberg, *improv instructor, Players' Workshop*
- Tom Cutler, *vice president, Leo Burnett USA*
- Mary Beth Erickson, *improv instructor, Players' Workshop*
- Margarita Geleske, *vice president, Leo Burnett USA*
- Maurice Geracht, *English professor, College of the Holy Cross*
- Jackie Hart, *dir., volunteer srvcs., Children's Memorial Med. Ctr.*
- Joel Hochberger, *manager of training, Leo Burnett USA*
- Amy Hohulin, *recruitment director, Leo Burnett USA*
- Ted Jordan, *executive vice president (retired), Leo Burnett USA*
- Claudia Koonz, *history professor, Duke University*
- Charles Locurto, *psychology professor, College of the Holy Cross*
- Cynthia Mah, *account supervisor, Leo Burnett USA*
- David P. Murphy, *improv instructor, Players' Workshop*
- Andy and Kristen Mercker, *video production/marketing professionals*
- Lisa Orman, *freelance writer/editor*
- Jan Perry, *public relations professional, Jan Perry Enterprises*
- Dave Polston, *marketing executive, PepsiCo./KFC*
- Steve Schildwachter, *account director, Impact (FCB/True North)*
- Joanne Sells, *sales professional*
- Ted Simon, *vice president (retired), Leo Burnett USA*
- Todd Townsend, *account supervisor, Leo Burnett USA*
- Steve Vineberg, *drama professor, College of the Holy Cross*

People who completed the picture

Other professionals who shared their time and insights.

> Colleen Boscelli, *DDB Needham*
> Pat Cafferata, *Young & Rubicam*
> Ellie Callison, *Leo Burnett USA*
> Kathy Deptula, *University of Evansville (Indiana)*
> Dan Fox, *Foote, Cone & Belding*
> Bob Hall, *Grant/Jacoby*
> Vera McRae, *David Cravitz/CME*
> Eileen Obeda, *Tatham Euro RSCG*
> Roland Ruble, *Crummer Graduate School of Business*
> Marty Sherrod, *Bayer, Bess, Vanderwarker*
> Bob Vogel, *Foote, Cone & Belding*

People who encouraged me

Throughout my life, these friends had the compassion, courage, and persistence to remind me of my potential when I didn't always believe it myself:

> Mary Balice
> David Brody
> Barbara and Stefan Ferm,
> Fr. Michael Ford, S.J.
> Mary Gebelien
> Heather Green
> Amy Harris
> Jackie Hart
> Chris Hennes
> Fr. Joseph LaBran, S.J.
> Ross Parr
> Christina Ranvik
> Rhonda Russell
> Melissa Stone
> Casey and Terry Sullivan
> Michéle Szafranski
> Tom Tillisch
> Harrison Vickers
> Harry and Irene Wilson

People who surprised me along the way

The unexpected, but welcome, contributors who gave me energy when I needed it most. Most of these people work in completely unrelated fields. I never dreamt they would have any interest in the project. A very special mention goes to 12-year-old **Michael Sholl**, a sixth-grader at Washburne Junior High in Winnetka, Illinois. Michael was so excited about the book that he offered to proofread it for typographical errors. Thanks, Michael.

Another special mention goes to **Jerald Durkin** at *JAR DESIGN* in Chicago. Before this book was printed, we completely redesigned the layout. Jerry and his team came through with top-notch work on extremely short notice. Thank you. Thank you. Thank you.

> Deanna Capps, *nurse, Columbus Hospital*
> Debbie Day, *software developer/consultant*
> Miriam Disman, *volunteer srvs., Children's Memorial Med. Ctr.*
> Greg Jordan, *attorney, Michael T. Hannafan & Associates*
> Kate Neavolls, *child life specialist, Children's Memorial Med. Ctr.*
> Ken Nicholson, *software consultant/founder, Systems Live*
> Connie Oswald, *special education teacher*
> Dave Penzell, *direct marketing consultant*
> Heidi Schlumpf, *associate editor, The New World*
> Mary Beth Tuohy, *Environmental Protection Agency*

People who made me smile

These are the people who made writing this book so much fun. Special thanks in this category goes to Mason, Suzi, Amanda, Julie, Stacy, Michelle, and everyone at the ***Bourgeois Pig***—one of the coolest coffee and sandwich shops in Chicago.

> Stephanie, Rich, Catherine, and Tony Bova
> Emery, Bobby, and Leigh Davis
> Sue and Ray Davis
> Diane DeMars
> Mary Economidy
> Penny Eller
> Jennifer Fondrevay
> Kathleen Gold
> The Joyce Family
> Marissa, Zara, Dan, Avril, and Hersch Klaff
> Brett, Bob and Mary Krugman
> KC, Becky, Zach, and Dillon Nagle
> The Sholl Family
> Catherine D. Sullivan
> David, Terry, and Sandy Wilson

People who inspired me

Each person, in his or her own way, has had a significant positive impact on the person I've become.

> Joe Almon, *floor trader, Chicago Board of Trade*
> Tami and Martin Block, *advertising research professionals*
> Brian Callahan, *floor trader, Chicago Board of Trade*
> Bruce Crown, *investor*
> Dan Delaney, *senior vice president, PaineWebber*
> Holly Dickens, *designer/founder, Holly Dickens Design*
> Jerry Dow, *account supervisor, Leo Burnett USA*
> Steve Ennen, *general manager/WUSN-FM, Infinity Broadcasting*
> Wilbert Jones, *chef, author of "The New Soul Food Cookbook"*
> Alex Kroll, *copywriter, Price-Webber*
> Ashley Landess, *freelance direct marketing copywriter*
> Scott and Connie Mastro, *option/futures traders*
> Tony McClintock, *teacher*
> Alan Miller, *band director, William B. Ogden Elementary School*
> Maureen Schmidt, *teacher (retired), William B. Ogden*
> Pamela Serp, *graphic designer, Capps Studio*
> Michael Selverian, *senior vice president, Cooper Neff & Associates*
> Craig Siegler, *venture capitalist, Siegler Corporation*
> Carrie Simpson, *vocalist/student*
> Pamela Smith, *Starlight Foundation*
> Chris Stewart, *chairperson/Wish List Auxiliary*
> Bruce Tate, *poet/writer (and manager at Tower Records Chicago)*
> Jill Thackeray, *print production, Leo Burnett USA*
> Brian J. Trausch, *floor trader, Chicago Board Options Exchange*

And, of course, special thanks to my mom, dad, sisters (ML and Clare), and brothers (Bill, John, and Matt)—the best family anyone could have. Without their encouragement, generosity, and patience, this book would not exist.

PREFACE

The unmet needs of the educated

With legions of college students entering the work force every year, competition for entry-level jobs is intense. A college degree simultaneously qualifies its holder for everything and nothing. In this sense, the degree is invaluable and worthless. As my grandmother puts it: "Your diploma and a bus token will get you downtown."

When it comes to job hunting, college and graduate students probably need the most help. They are also least likely to receive it. Unfortunately, society does more to help nonprofessionals than it does to help the educated.

Vocational high schools, secretarial schools, and truck driving schools are but a few of the limitless options available to the American working class. What we lack is an effective way to help educated people pursue executive positions. The message is silent but clear:

"You are smart enough to be where you are, figure it out yourself."

In the absence of effective training, aspiring professionals must rely on natural ability, luck, and resourcefulness. As a result, a disproportionate number of graduates accept jobs that are not the best match for their interests and abilities. Fortunately, there's hope. By recognizing and demonstrating your potential, you can learn to market yourself effectively. This book will show you how.

THERE'S NEVER TIME TO DO IT RIGHT. BUT THERE'S ALWAYS TIME TO DO IT OVER.

—*MESKIMEN'S LAW*

Introduction

How this Book is Different

Climbing Your Way to the Bottom is based on the theory that your relationship with a potential employer is almost exactly the same as the relationships that exist between products and consumers. There is only one key difference: In the job search, you are both product and salesperson.

The job seekers most likely to benefit from this book have already focused on a particular career—whatever that may be. If this describes you, congratulations. You are taking the right steps. The fact that you are reading this suggests that you are open-minded, eager to learn, and willing to challenge yourself. These are valuable qualities to any employer.

> WORLDLY WISDOM TEACHES THAT IT IS BETTER FOR THE REPUTATION TO FAIL CONVENTIONALLY THAN TO SUCCEED UNCONVENTIONALLY.
>
> —JOHN MAYNARD KEYNES

What if I have no idea what I want to do?

If you find yourself in this category, there may be a few issues to address before you begin. For example, have you answered the following questions?

- What is the best use of my talents?
- Should I pursue an advanced degree?
- Should I relocate?

If not, I suggest that you start by reading *What Color Is Your Parachute?* by Richard Nelson Bolles. The exercises and questions in that book will guide you through the preliminary steps.

What this book will do

The strategies outlined in this book will help you:

- communicate effectively in writing
- prepare for interviews
- present yourself in interviews
- seek and be open to criticism

- maintain perspective
- believe in yourself
- secure a challenging position

Many of the examples and anecdotes in this book are advertising/marketing specific. I adopted this approach for a number of reasons:

- The basic principles of marketing (e.g., product positioning) apply to any job search.
- Advertising/marketing positions are among the most sought after jobs for college grads. (Leo Burnett receives 10,000 résumés every year for account management alone.) If you understand how to position yourself against these odds, you probably have what it takes to compete in any field.

Focusing on a particular industry also makes it is possible to explore, in-depth, how the same candidates can reposition themselves to appeal to companies with different needs. In other words, modify the approach to match your area of interest. With a few weeks of focused preparation, you can sell yourself into almost any job. Why? Because that's a few weeks longer than your competition usually spends.

Using this book

If you read this book passively, nod your head occasionally, and put it away, you will have wasted your time. Treat it as a textbook. Give yourself homework assignments. Scribble notes in the margin. You are both teacher and student. Although this book requires effort and self-discipline, I have included questions and examples to help you prepare. Whether you know it or not, you have what it takes to compete. You are obviously curious, driven, and committed to self-improvement. These are important and relatively rare qualities. Nurture them.

Marketing yourself

Despite what you might think, your ability to get a job has little to do with experience or intelligence. You don't need a résumé overflowing with internships and degrees. Instead, you must take the time to learn to market yourself. This is a lifelong process with serious short- and long-term implications. It is not a bizarre punishment reserved for those who never find themselves in the right place at the right time.

To market yourself effectively, you must match your skills with the needs of a potential employer. This way, the job search can be quick and relatively painless. On the other hand, if you don't know what the company needs, you probably don't know what you have to offer. In this case, you will be relying on luck to guide your personal and professional satisfaction. This is a great recipe for disappointment. Worse, your job search will drag on indefinitely until you accept a position for which you are overqualified.

A personal marketing plan

A marketing plan, whether it's for a person, product, or service—must include the following:

- product analysis
- target analysis
- category analysis
- competitive analysis
- communication plan

In the job search, you are the product; the potential employer is the consumer; your cover letter and résumé are interest-generating print ads; and your interview is the sales call in which both parties assess whether or not the product (you) fits the consumer's needs (the available position).

In some cases, there are significant differences between companies with respect to the qualities they seek. Take time to identify these differences. Your value will be measured by your ability to meet the needs of the employer.

Without a marketing plan, most candidates make the hiring decision an easy one. They have no idea what the company needs or what they, as candidates, have to offer. Some don't even know why they want to work in a given field. With so many other people competing for the same position, no interviewer has time to search for a spark of potential. It must be apparent. Of those who don't succeed, few ever find out why. Most don't even think to ask.

Ongoing efforts

Just as the marketing effort does not end when a customer makes a purchase decision, your marketing effort should not end when you get an offer or rejection. The challenge has just begun.

Beyond rejection

Unfortunately, the best preparation may not spare you from disappointment. Should this happen, keep looking for opportunities to improve. Never stop believing in yourself. This is an active process. As a wise person once said:

"Disappointment is when you only hope things get better."

PART 1

Creating a Marketing Plan for Yourself

The Product: *Learning to sell yourself*

The Category: *Careers and competitors*

Creating Awareness

FEAR IS THE THIEF OF DREAMS.

—RONALD THORNTON

CHAPTER 1

The Product
Learning to sell yourself

The Paradox of Preparation

It has always amazed me that people will spend several hundred dollars and weeks of their lives taking SAT, LSAT, and GMAT preparation courses, but they won't spend more than a weekend on cover letters, résumés, and interview preparation. Then they treat the job search as a black and white proposition—either they get the job or they don't. Sadly, this ignores is the enormous distinction between just missing the cut and never coming close.

A rejection is not the job market's way of saying "you aren't good enough." A rejection is nothing more than a warning that you aren't marketing yourself effectively. If you don't heed the warnings and uncover opportunities for improvement, you will repeat the same mistakes.

IT'S NEVER WISE TO LEAP A CHASM IN TWO BOUNDS.

—*CHINESE PROVERB*

EVERY MOMENT SPENT PLANNING SAVES TWO OR THREE MOMENTS OF EXECUTION.

—*HYRUM SMITH (ATTRIBUTED)*

The typical scenario

You interview. You wait. You think about calling. You wait a little longer. Finally, you call. The company has no news. A few weeks pass. At last a postcard arrives:

> "Thank you for expressing an interest in our company. Unfortunately, your background and abilities do not match our needs at this time. Best of luck in your job search."

If you are a college student, a letter like this is usually good for a free beer at the campus pub. On the other hand, if you are in the middle of an extensive job search, this may be one more in an unbroken string of rejections. Either way, it says nothing more than: "You didn't get the job."

In our litigious and vengeful society, there is a tendency to couch every phrase in the most nebulous and inoffensive terms. As a result, the most common explanation for rejections (i.e., "Your talents don't meet our needs") is meaningless.

Another approach

Given the intense competition in the job market, it's unrealistic to expect that you or anyone else can avoid rejection. I didn't. No one I know did. And you probably won't either. Instead, your probability for success is a function of your willingness to extract value from rejection and failure. Putting your ego on the line—particularly in front of a company that has already rejected you—probably seems like a stressful, time-consuming diversion. What makes this approach worthwhile is the impact it can have on your effectiveness.

From here to your future

When the distance between your present situation and your goals is measured in time, the shortest distance is not always a straight line. A jagged route may be the shortest. Consider the following diagram:

A — — — — — — — — — **B**
(unemployment)   *(dream job)*

If Point A is unemployment and Point B is your dream job, the straight line between A and B would seem to be the shortest path. If you are already proficient at marketing yourself, perhaps it is. Otherwise, it most definitely is not.

Without preparation and practice, a straight line between A and B cannot exist. A more accurate visual representation looks like this:

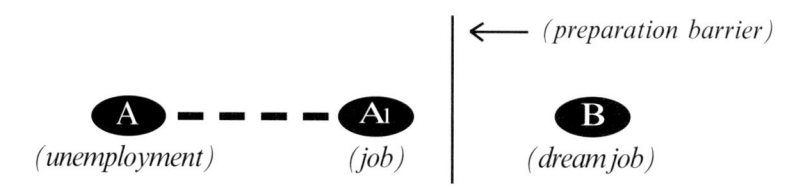

                                             ← *(preparation barrier)*

A — — — **A₁**   **B**
(unemployment)   *(job)*   *(dream job)*

To get beyond the barrier, your journey from Point A to Point B must include:

- A thorough self-analysis
    - Who are you?
    - What do you want to do?
    - Why do you want to do it?
    - Why would you be good at it?

- A personal marketing plan
    - self-analysis
    - target/industry analysis
    - competitive analysis
    - focused selling message

In this case, the shortest distance between Point A and Point B is:

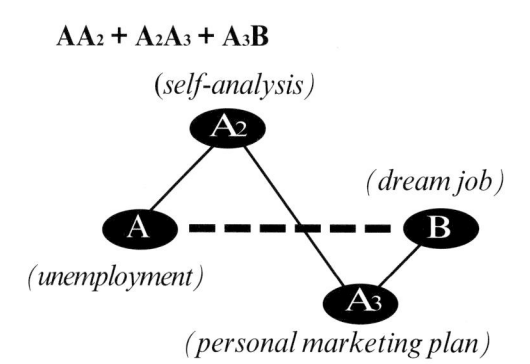

AA$_2$ + A$_2$A$_3$ + A$_3$B

```
            (self-analysis)
                 A₂
                 ●
                / \
               /   \    (dream job)
              /     \
         A  ●━ ━ ━ ━ ━● B
  (unemployment)  \   /
                   \ /
                    ●
                    A₃
            (personal marketing plan)
```

When distance is measured in time, or as a function of the probability for success, the following is true:

AA$_2$ + A$_2$A$_3$ + A$_3$B < AB

Fortunately, this is almost all the math you need to know.

An ounce of preparation. . .

The commitment that you must make to preparation may not excite you, but it's better than the alternative—settling for the wrong job.

A FRIEND IS ONE WHO SEES THROUGH YOU AND STILL ENJOYS THE VIEW.

—*WILMA ASKINAS*

KEEP GROWING, SILENTLY AND EARNESTLY THROUGH YOUR WHOLE DEVELOPMENT; YOU COULDN'T DISTURB IT ANY MORE VIOLENTLY THAN BY LOOKING OUTSIDE AND WAITING FOR OUTSIDE ANSWERS TO QUESTIONS THAT ONLY YOUR INNERMOST FEELING, IN YOUR QUIETEST HOUR, CAN PERHAPS ANSWER.

—*RAINER MARIA RILKE, "LETTERS TO A YOUNG POET"*

Self-Analysis

Although countless pages have been written about job hunting, much of the information is hopelessly inadequate. Read enough on the subject and you might think appearance counts for more than presentation. It doesn't.

The key is effective preparation. This includes, but is not limited to, collecting as much information as possible about the industry, the company, and the position. In addition, much of your time should be spent matching your qualifications with the company's expectations. In other words, give the company specific reasons to hire you. You have something to offer. Tell them what it is.

Finding your niche

It often happens that the best marketing opportunities involve positioning a product for a niche market. Likewise, the way you define and redefine yourself can play a role in your job search. What interests or experiences enhance your professional value?

- Are you fluent in a foreign language?

- Do you have a particular area of expertise?

- Which companies would value what you have to offer?

The experience doesn't have to be exotic. If you grew up on a farm and earned an MBA, you might highlight the discipline and independence you gained from farming. In addition, your knowledge of farming combined with your business education would probably be invaluable to agricultural companies and the marketing firms that represent them. Anyone can get an MBA. Not everyone grows up on a farm. Fewer still do both.

Do you know yourself?

Conceptually, it seems like you should already be an expert in this area. Nevertheless, this is where most candidates fall apart. A few well-chosen questions by an interviewer can easily demonstrate inadequate preparation. To be unconvincing and unprepared to deal with questions about who you are and why you want to work in a particular industry is no different than sending yourself a rejection letter on the corporate letterhead of your choice.

I cannot stress enough how important preparation is. Think about every aspect of your life. Use the questions at the end of this chapter to stimulate your thinking. Take detailed notes. Know exactly who you are, what you like, what you want to do, and why you want to do it.

- How would you answer each question in one or two sentences?

- Given the chance to elaborate, what would you say?

- What other issues or personality characteristics play a key role in defining who you are?

A complete and thoughtful self-analysis is the first step in creating your personal marketing plan. While you may never be asked every question on the following pages, each, in its own way, will help you to understand the person you are today.

QUESTIONS FOR SELF-ANALYSIS

Family/Growing Up
- What role did you play in your family?
- What was good/bad about your family relationships? How did this impact you?
- How has the marital status of your parents impacted the person you have become?
- Did you grow up in one place or did you move several times?
- If your family relocated, how did you handle the adjustment?
- What did you like best about growing up?
- If you could relive one day from your childhood, which one would it be? Why?
- What would you change about your childhood if you could?
- What would you change about your life?
- What childhood incident(s) most affected you?

School
- Think back to grade school, high school, college and/or graduate school. What did you enjoy most about each school/experience?
- How did you choose the college/graduate school that you attended?
- If you could change anything about any school you attended, what would it be and how might you go about doing it?
- If you transferred, why? How did you make the decision? What are the positive and negative aspects of this decision? Looking back, how do you feel about the decision? What might you do differently?
- Overall, was school enjoyable and challenging or easy and boring?

Social Interaction
- Why do people like you?
- How well do you get along with others?
- Do people like you instantly or does it take time to get to know you?
- What reasons would people have to dislike you?
- Do you prefer to work by yourself or as part of a team?
- Do you do any volunteer work or community service? If so, what do you like best about it?
- Are you more comfortable as a leader or as a follower?
- What qualities do you value in a friend? Spouse? Coworker?

(Continued on next page)

QUESTIONS FOR SELF-ANALYSIS *(continued)*

Interests/Accomplishments
- What are your hobbies?
- How do you spend your free time?
- What would be your ideal vacation?
- What accomplishment gives you the most pride?

Job History/Preferences
- Have you ever had a job?
- For each job answer these questions:
    - Why did you take it?
    - How did you get it?
    - What did you learn?
    - What were your responsibilities?
- Would you consider relocating?
- Would you like to work overseas? If so, what relevant skills can you offer an employer?
- What did you like about your previous job(s)? What didn't you like?

Motivations/Goals
- How do you stay motivated?
- If you could spend your life doing anything (career-oriented) and money wasn't an issue, what would you do?
- If you could only accomplish one goal in life, what would it be?
- What, if anything, is worth dying for?
- Why do you want to work in a particular industry?
- What other careers have you considered?
- How often do you identify and prioritize short-, medium-, and long-term goals?
- How does your mind work? Are you particularly analytical? Resourceful? Strategic? Creative?
- What are your professional objectives?

(Continued on next page)

QUESTIONS FOR SELF-ANALYSIS (*continued*)

Work Ethic
- Are you organized? Detail-oriented? Punctual?
- What would previous employers identify as your greatest strengths? Greatest opportunities for improvement?
- When handling involved projects, would you rather focus on the big picture or manage the details? Why?

Personality/Creativity
- What do you like most about yourself?
- What are some of your best ideas?
- If you could invent anything, what would it be?
- What is the most important lesson you have learned?
- What are your personal objectives?
- What is your most prized possession?

Problem-Solving
- What are the biggest challenges you have overcome?
    - What steps did you take?
    - What did you learn?
    - Given the chance to start over, how might you handle the situations differently?
- How did the outcome impact others?
    - Did you create a win-win situation for all parties?
    - Was anyone left feeling powerless or disappointed?
    - Are you satisfied with the results?
    - How might you improve your performance?
- What challenges have you faced that remain unresolved?
    - What opportunities do you have to improve the situation?
    - Are you taking action to resolve the issues? Why or why not?

CHAPTER 2

The Category
Careers and Competitors

Target Analysis

Knowing where you want to work does not lessen the effort required for the industry analysis. You still need a solid grasp of the differences and similarities between companies to convince interviewers that you have done your homework. Factors to consider include:

- recruiting objectives
- size
- reputation
- clients, products, or services

Recruiting objectives

Different companies have different recruiting objectives. Although two companies may handle similar products or services, differences (e.g., clients) will always exist. This impacts the corporate culture and, ultimately, staffing requirements.

In preparing this book, I conducted an informal telephone survey of advertising recruiters. For the most part, these people didn't consider their objectives unusual. Nevertheless, the differences were extreme. The qualities sought by one agency might be meaningless—even detrimental—in the eyes of another.

In some cases, the differences can be attributed to the company's expectations about the future of the industry. One CEO described the perfect entry-level account person as creative and entrepreneurial. She based her preferences on the rapid changes already impacting her clients. In order to properly service these clients, she actively recruits risk-takers. In contrast, agencies with more conservative clients are often more risk-averse.

While it is possible for a savvy applicant to tailor a presentation to address companies with conflicting requirements, that misses the point. Denying your preferences to gain employment is shortsighted and hazardous.

FEW PEOPLE DO BUSINESS WELL WHO DO NOTHING ELSE.

—*EARL OF CHESTERFIELD*

Clarify the company's objectives

When you are unsure about the needs of a particular company, make phone calls rather than assumptions. First, call the human resources department and state your objective:

> "I am interested in learning more about a position at your company. Specifically, I'd like to know what qualities you look for in entry-level applicants. Do you have a brochure that describes your recruiting objectives?"

If the company doesn't have the information, politely ask:

> "Is there anyone—perhaps a first-year employee—who might be able to address this question? I'll only take a minute of their time."

Size

Size is relative. To one person, a large but close-knit family atmosphere may seem small relative to a multi-billion dollar global company. To another, it might seem enormous. For this reason, I will not attempt to establish artificial cutoff points between small, midsize, and large companies.

At a smaller company, you may have more opportunity for direct involvement and access to top management. On the other hand, a large company can offer a wider range of departments, resources, and job opportunities. The correct choice is the one that appeals to you.

Reputation

If you must rely on the trade press to assess an company's reputation, use more than one article and publication. This will balance the impact of writers who, at times, are less than objective. Start by comparing the facts:

- clients, products, or services
- annual growth rate (company and industry)
- employee attrition

Then, use a more qualitative approach:

- What is the company's vision for long-term growth/profitability?

    - What will fuel future growth?

    - Has the company won/lost any business?

- How well is the company positioned in the global marketplace?

Much of the information above can be accessed through the trade press and company promotional literature. The trade press is a good source for industry news, marketing trends, salary surveys, and other general information. If you have trouble locating specific information, ask the reference librarian at your local library.

Clients, Products, or Services

In general, almost all of a company's income comes from the sale of its products. In a service business, such as advertising, most of the revenue comes from the sale of its clients' products. For this reason, it makes sense to find a company with products and clients you would be proud to represent. In his book *Ogilvy on Advertising*, David Ogilvy describes going to great lengths to support client products. Ogilvy, who was known for his impeccable appearance, stocked his wardrobe with suits from Sears Roebuck & Company—a longtime client.

The issue of supporting client products is especially important if you hope to work in an industry that promotes the manufacturing, distribution, and advertising of controversial items. Would you have any difficulty promoting or representing beer, wine, liquor, condoms, cigarettes, sports cars, or defense contractors? In no way am I suggesting that you, as an employee of a company, dedicate your life to smoking, drinking, or anything else you find objectionable. However, if you are employed in a particular industry, you should support—at least passively—the responsible promotion and distribution of its products.

I HAVE ALWAYS BEEN NAIVELY GUIDED BY THE PRINCIPLE THAT IF WE DO NOT BELIEVE IN THE PRODUCTS WE ADVERTISE STRONGLY ENOUGH TO USE THEM OURSELVES, OR AT LEAST TO GIVE THEM A REAL TRY, WE ARE NOT COMPLETELY HONEST WITH OURSELVES IN ADVERTISING THEM TO OTHERS. THE VERY LEAST WE CAN DO IS TO REMAIN NEUTRAL.

—*LEO BURNETT*

> *A WISE MAN WILL MAKE MORE OPPORTUNITIES THAN HE FINDS.*
>
> —FRANCIS BACON

Creating Other Opportunities

As you evaluate career options, look beyond the obvious industry-specific opportunities. For example, if you are a truly entrepreneurial soul, you might gain experience helping small local businesses in your field of interest. This is especially applicable to anyone interested in marketing. Unlike doctors and lawyers, marketers do not need a license or an advanced degree to practice. You don't even need original ideas. The desire and ability to execute business building programs is enough.

Before contacting anyone, take the time to understand the business, the consumer, the competition, and the market opportunity. Then, write a letter of introduction describing what you have to offer and why it is valuable. A letter is better than a phone call or personal visit because it shows more effort. Anyone can make a phone call. Not everyone can write a convincing letter.

This strategy can work anywhere. If you haven't graduated from college, you might even use it to find a summer job. If you come up empty-handed, remember to give yourself credit for the effort. When you do finally succeed, you will have the extra sense of accomplishment that only comes from creating something from nothing.

Selling by listening

Once you have arranged a meeting with a business owner, you will probably be anxious to share your ideas. Enthusiasm is important. Listening is even more important. One of my first meetings as a freelance consultant was with the CEO of a development-stage software company. Once we shook hands, he opened the conversation saying: "I have no particular agenda." He proceeded to spend the next thirty minutes describing his hopes, dreams, and visions. At that point, selling myself was easy because I knew exactly what he needed. There is no substitute for active listening.

Your Competition

Once you have completed a thorough self-analysis and target analysis, start thinking about the competition. To market yourself effectively, you must know the relative strengths of the competition and position yourself accordingly.

> *IF YOU COMPARE YOURSELF WITH OTHERS, YOU MAY BECOME VAIN OR BITTER, FOR ALWAYS THERE WILL BE GREATER AND LESSER PERSONS THAN YOURSELF.*
>
> —DESIDERATA

Recent college graduates

Some companies prefer candidates with bachelor's degrees because they:

- start at lower salaries than candidates who have advanced degrees

- are energetic/eager to learn

    - Without full-time corporate experience, recent college grads are seen as blank slates who can be shaped, molded, and trained to the company's specifications.

Master's in Business Administration (MBA)

For college graduates interested in some aspect of business, the stiffest competition may come from the top MBA programs. These applicants differ in that they often have previous work experience and specialized business training (e.g., marketing, finance, and accounting). Theoretically, MBAs have the tools to make immediate contributions. This may be attractive to companies, but it doesn't come without cost. MBAs command significantly higher salaries.

Positioning yourself against the competition

At some point, you may encounter an interviewer who challenges your level of education relative to other candidates. Should this happen, focus on what you have to offer. Avoid direct comparisons. If you are asked specifically for a comparison, highlight the positive. Whatever you do, don't answer the question *"Why shouldn't we hire them?"* Instead, answer the question *"Why should we hire you?"* Companies hire "them" all the time.

Being clear on the relative merits of your education is particularly important if you have an advanced degree. If the company will be paying you a premium salary, know why you are worth it.

CHAPTER 3

Creating Awareness

When launching a new product or service, companies often rely on the power of advertising. Whether they use a print ad, commercial, sales brochure, or billboard, the goal is the same—to generate interest. Your résumé and cover letter are no different. You are the product. The prospective employer is the consumer. Your goal is to generate job offers.

Understanding the Concepts

If the thought of selling yourself in writing or in person traumatizes you, take a moment to reflect on any associations you make with the following words or phrases:

- cover letters
- résumés
- interviews

How do you feel when you hear these words? How might you define each? Unless these concepts are completely unfamiliar, you already have at least a vague understanding or interpretation. What is that?

Although fear and uncertainty are common reactions, many people are not comfortable admitting it. Nevertheless, an honest assessment is critical. Ignoring or denying the truth—no matter how unattractive it may be—has an even uglier impact on personal effectiveness.

Facing fear and uncertainty

Use a separate sheet of paper for each fear-inducing concept you plan to explore. Reflecting on one concept at a time, write down every thought that comes to mind. Once you have a complete list, ask yourself:

ONLY PASSIONS, GREAT PASSIONS, CAN ELEVATE THE SOUL TO GREAT THINGS.

—DENIS DIDEROT

WE MAY BECOME THE MAKERS OF OUR FATE WHEN WE HAVE CEASED TO POSE AS ITS PROPHETS.

—KARL POPPER

"If this _____ was a ruthless critic who knew everything about me, what might he or she say?"
(cover letter, résumé, interview, etc.)

Another question to consider is:

"If people really knew me, would they still like me?"

Facing your own insecurity can be a wonderful and liberating experience. It's also an important part of a comprehensive self-assessment. Another way to access the same information is to reflect on these questions:

- What do you fear most?

- What do you hope the world never finds out about you?

- Do you see yourself as:

    - inept?

    - inadequate?

    - unqualified?

    - unreliable?

    - insecure?

    - unfocused?

    - a hindrance/burden to others?

    - a failure?

To show how this works, I'll recreate what would have happened if I had done this exercise as a college senior. My ruthless critic would have been the blank sheet of paper that I hoped would become my cover letter. Given a voice, it would have said:

"Rob, how can you possibly create me? You don't really know what I am. You've never written anything like me before. And you haven't even met the person you're sending me to. People will see right through this. You don't have a chance."

Through this thought process I became my own worst enemy. In effect, I created insurmountable obstacles in the form of unrealistically high expectations. Had I somehow succeeded, I would have done so in spite of myself. Countless others torture themselves the same way. Don't be one of them.

When objectives become expectations

People who set and achieve lofty objectives often find that they become expectations rather than goals. When this happens, only two outcomes are possible: disappointment and non-disappointment. Disappointment—the failure to meet our own expectations—occurs when we rob ourselves of the freedom to make mistakes. Non-disappointment describes the state of being that exists when the expected results are achieved. A healthier response would be a sense of accomplishment, satisfaction, and inner peace. If the best you can hope for is non-disappointment, you haven't given yourself much reason to live.

Ultimately, we have a choice. We can punish ourselves for mistakes or we can accept them as a natural part of life. As it happens, the ability to accept our humanity—and by definition, our imperfection—can be a wonderful source of the strength we need to ask for help.

I HAVE MADE THIS LETTER LONGER THAN USUAL, BECAUSE I LACK THE TIME TO MAKE IT SHORT.

—PASCAL

Cover Letters

A cover letter is not a professional-looking Post-It note attached to your résumé with the message: *"Hey, check this out. I'd really like to work for you."* Nor are they afterthoughts. Cover letters and résumés work together as distinct parts of the same communication.

Unlike your résumé, every word of your cover letter will be read. Ideally, it convinces the reader that you are worth interviewing—even before he or she reads the résumé. Although my feelings are far from universal, I view cover letters as more distinctive and revealing than résumés. A convincing, well-written cover letter will almost always grab my attention. The writer is almost always articulate and intelligent—or at least resourceful enough to seek qualified assistance. In contrast, an ill-conceived, poorly written cover letter makes a powerful negative statement—even when it accompanies a better-than-average résumé. To be blunt, a person who cannot write persuasively will not make my team.

The typical (and worthless) cover letter

"The reputation you have developed as a discriminating consumer makes you an attractive target for our product. At this time, our product is in the development stage. It has not been tested. Nor has it been approved for use. However, if we could interest you in using it, your endorsement would be instrumental in improving its marketability and enhancing its reputation. Please call me at your earliest convenience to discuss your valued assistance."

The paragraph above is the advertising equivalent of a typical cover letter. Unfortunately, the approach is closer to begging than marketing because it focuses exclusively on what the recipient can do for the writer. It should be the other way around. Recruiters know why they are important to you. What they don't know is why you are important to them.

Write the cover letter as if it were your only opportunity to market yourself. Then, evaluate what you have written from the point of view of a recruiter. Make sure it communicates potential. If you haven't marketed yourself effectively, don't expect to get an interview. Marketing recruiters, in particular, are unlikely to interview anyone who isn't clear on the concept.

What is marketing?

According to Philip Kotler, Professor of Marketing at Northwestern University and noted authority on the subject, marketing is:

> "A social and managerial process by which individuals and groups obtain what they need and want through creating and exchanging products and value with others" (*Marketing Management: Analysis, Planning, Implementation, and Control* [New Jersey: Prentice-Hall, 1988, 6th ed.], 3).

"Process" and "exchange" are two of the most important words in this definition. The process typically occurs as a form of communication (e.g., print ad, negotiation, letter). Likewise, an exchange can be goods for services, money for services, or money for goods. For an exchange to occur, the buyer and seller must each believe they will be better off having made the exchange.

Marketing lessons from the homeless

My favorite example of effective marketing came from a panhandler who achieved the impossible. He convinced a passing motorist to break her self-imposed rule of not giving money to street people. Strangely, he didn't use fear, coercion, or any of the usual weapons of choice. Instead, a large cardboard sign shared his only assets: honesty, sincerity, and a sense of humor. It read simply:

"Who am I kidding? All I really need is a beer."

If a panhandler can market himself effectively on a soiled cardboard box, just think what you can do in a letter. Don't force yourself to be creative. Just answer two questions:

- Why am I worth interviewing?
- What do I have to offer?

Too often, candidates focus on the reputation of the company and its resources without regard to the skills they will contribute to the team. Tell me why I should interview you. Make me believe you have potential.

Content

An effective cover letter communicates the following in less than one page:

- your objective
- direct comparisons between your skills and the company's needs
- a date you will call to follow-up

Your objective

Your reason for writing should be clear within the first few sentences. For example:

- to request an informational interview.
- to seek an entry-level position.

Direct comparisons between your skills and the company's needs

Show that you have done your homework. You know what qualities the company values in entry-level employees. Give examples that demonstrate your potential in these areas.

Think of each example in the cover letter as a topic sentence supported with specifics in the résumé. The cover letter makes sense of your experience and relates it to the challenges of the position. The résumé is a reference for those who want more information.

A date you will call to follow-up

At the end of your letter, let the person know you will be calling in the next few weeks. For example:

> "I will call your office in two weeks to see if we can set up an interview at your convenience."

Allow at least ten days before you call. If you are unable to make contact, leave your name and ask the secretary to suggest a time you might call again. If you are particularly difficult to reach, consider getting a stand-alone voice mail. This may be the best $10 (or less) a month you ever spend.

Proofreading

It disturbs me that I even have to mention this, but your letter should be concise, grammatically correct, and convincing. Otherwise, for the good of the planet, it better be biodegradable.

Before you send any business correspondence, it's a good idea to have another human being look over your work. SpellCheck is great, but it doesn't catch everything. Just ask my editors.

SAMPLE COVER LETTER
(No Reason to Believe)

Mr. John Butler
Product Development
Illinois Superconductor
Mt. Prospect, IL 60056

Dear Mr. Butler:

In this age of parity products and decreasing profits, only companies that stay on the cutting-edge of technology can remain competitive. That's why Illinois Superconductor will be so successful.

What attracts me to Illinois Superconductor is the company's commitment to high-temperature superconducting technology as it relates to the cellular market. The successful field tests that the company has performed in partnership with Ameritech, Southwestern Bell, and other base station operators suggests a bright future for the company's technology in general and SpectrumMaster filters in particular. For these reasons, I am confident that Illinois Superconductor would provide a wonderful opportunity for me to work and learn.

Enclosed you will find a copy of my résumé. I look forward to hearing from you.

Sincerely,

Richard Ashton

General impression: The writer demonstrates a limited understanding of the company, yet fails to provide an objective or a reason to believe he is worth interviewing.

Paragraph 1: The writer should have included his objective (e.g., to apply for a position in product development, field sales, etc.).

Paragraph 2: Here, the writer should have drawn specific parallels between his potential, his experience or knowledge, and the company's recruiting objectives. The recipient doesn't care what kind of an opportunity he might provide for the writer. In contrast, the writer should make it clear what he has to offer the employer. He did not.

Closing: The writer should never leave it up to the recipient to follow-up.

SAMPLE COVER LETTER

Mr. James Tolhurst
Senior Account Executive
Kroll Communications
Chicago, IL 60611

Dear Mr. Tolhurst:

I am writing to express my interest in pursuing a career in account management with Kroll Communications. Enclosed you will find a copy of my résumé for your review.

I understand that you look for individuals who possess initiative, strategic problem-solving abilities, and communication skills. These are skills I have honed through my marketing internships at the Leukemia Research Foundation and Half Court Press.

Recognizing my passion for marketing, a vice president at the Leukemia Research Foundation invited me to participate in the strategic planning and implementation of their direct marketing programs. Later, I applied this knowledge to improve the direct response efforts at Half Court Press. As a result, the company is better able to track consumer purchase behavior. The company is also using this system to monitor the impact of specific marketing efforts at the retail level.

My experience in nonprofit and consumer-oriented marketing is a strong indicator of my potential at a company like Kroll Communications. I am particularly attracted to the company's focus on integrated marketing. The success of The Winnetka Brewery, Grizzly Bear Bottling and others is a strong testimony to the agency's strength and vision. These are just a few of the reasons I would be proud to contribute my skills to the Kroll team.

I will call you in two weeks to set up an interview at your convenience. Thank you for your time and consideration.

Sincerely,

Monika McMurtry

General impression: Overall, the writer does a good job explaining who she is, why she is writing, and how she has demonstrated important marketing skills.

Opportunity for improvement: This letter would be even stronger if the writer made direct comparisons between her skills and the agency's needs. Although she clearly has potential, she may have missed a critical skill (e.g., leadership) that Kroll values.

> *RULES AND MODELS DESTROY GENIUS AND ART.*
>
> —WILLIAM HAZLITT

> *BUILD A REPUTATION ON WHAT YOU DO—NOT ALL THE THINGS YOU INTEND TO.*
>
> —JACKIE DOUGLASS

Résumés

Unless you know exactly why a potential employer should be interested in you, don't bother to write a résumé. A résumé must have a reason for being apart from the vague desire to secure full-time employment.

For demonstration purposes, this section is built around a fictitious undergraduate named Emery McTell. Although you and Emery may not share the same professional objectives, you can learn a lot by applying the process to your own situation.

The biographical sketch provides an overview of the experiences from which Emery has to draw in creating a résumé and cover letter appropriate for advertising. Despite the fact that Emery has no prior full-time work experience, she has qualities that smart employers value—passion and initiative. Some people refer to this as a "fire in the belly." Others describe it as "a burning hunger." Whatever it is, she's got it.

In many respects, Emery's background is aspirational. For the truly hungry—the people who get the hard-to-get jobs—it is also achievable. It's important to notice that Emery's experience is a result of her own initiative. There isn't one experience listed that isn't achievable in your own life. It doesn't matter if your talents are not creatively, analytically, or strategically focused. With a little inspiration, you can market any ability or interest. And you'll almost certainly learn more on your own than you would in an internship with a Fortune 500 company. (Contrary to popular opinion, internships are not prerequisites for gainful employment. Most are glorified secretarial positions.)

While it isn't necessary to compare yourself point-for-point or award-for-award to Emery or anyone else, you should be able to identify and leverage your own unique selling points. The most difficult part of the process is the self-analysis. Once you have matched your skills with an employer's needs, the cover letter and résumé will flow naturally.

Employment history

Many job applicants are also under the erroneous impression that qualifications relate to past employment rather than personal accomplishment. These people would sooner apologize for their (lack of) employment history than sell themselves on raw talent. This insecurity has two negative consequences:

- Time that should be spent preparing is spent procrastinating.

- The résumé, when it is finally written, is a meaningless collection of facts that could apply to anyone—and sells no one.

This is particularly hazardous because the most notable achievements of recent graduates are rarely work-related. These people, in particular, should keep three facts in mind:

- Your history, whether it includes full-time employment or not, is just that—history. It is not an excuse for you, your behavior, or anything else. The past is only useful to the extent that it can be used to demonstrate potential.

- By definition, entry-level positions are filled by people who have no prior experience. People who have experience in a given field don't compete at the entry-level.

- Employers recruiting for entry-level positions are more interested in potential than experience.

Through the eyes of an interviewer

Starting now, forget everything you have heard or believe about résumés. In this section, we will examine the structure, assumptions, and details that make résumés ineffective. Then, we will begin with a blank page.

The exercises in this section are intended as a guide to focus your efforts. Notice that I used the word focus rather than dictate. The all-purpose, one-size-fits-all format is exactly the shortsighted approach that causes problems in the first place. As you work through the chapter, you may find the sample résumés intimidating. That's good. Like it or not, you will be competing against people who have accomplished more in a summer vacation than others do in a lifetime.

The most common résumé problems

Most résumés lack both individuality and focus. Like anyone who interviews people, I have seen hundreds of résumés. However, I can count on one hand the number of truly exceptional résumés that have crossed my desk. Sadly, there were more than a few gifted people camouflaged by their own unfocused presentation. On paper, they looked just like everybody else. I could bore you with statistics about how long the average interviewer spends reading a résumé, but I won't. Believe me, it's not long. Although it's likely that every word of your cover letter will be read, the same cannot be said of your résumé.

Individuality, as it relates to the résumé, is not a synonym for creativity. Rather, it is the degree to which the résumé positions the candidate as both unique and qualified. Upon seeing the résumé, the reader should think:

"There is no one in the world this could be except you."

Too often, the assessment can only be:

"This could be anybody in the world <u>including</u> you."

Biographical Sketch

Name: Emery Stephanie McTell
Age: 21
Sex: Female
Occupation: Student
  State University
  Major: Communications
  Minor: Psychology
  Graduation: This June

Extracurricular Activities:
State University Marketing Club
University Daily Newspaper
WAVO-FM

Career Objective: Advertising Account Management

Work Experience
Full-time: None
Part-time: Just For Fun Designs (1989-1991)
Spare Time Promotions (1990-Present)

Just For Fun Designs

During her freshman year in high school, Emery became interested in jewelry design. At first she made earrings, bracelets, and watchbands exclusively for herself and her friends. As more people wore the jewelry, demand increased. Before long, she found herself spending more time making jewelry just to keep pace with requests. Within 18 months, this activity generated $200 per week in profit. At peak efficiency, Emery only had to work three or four nights a week for two hours and one day every other weekend to meet demand.

The next year, Emery began selling her products to nearby stores under the name Just For Fun Designs. Since she no longer had direct contact with the customer, Emery enclosed a return postcard for people who wanted to be added to the mailing list. Whenever a new store began carrying Just For Fun products, people on the mailing list received an announcement. As her list of satisfied customers grew, so did her distribution network.

Spare Time Promotions

As it happened, Emery had as much fun marketing her products as she did making them. After reading a story about a six-year-old boy who sold bumper stickers to promote world peace, she wrote to local newspapers with her own story. Her objective was to create awareness so others stores might carry the products. It worked. When the local paper picked up the story, three additional stores asked to carry her products. Emery also began to receive calls from other artists and craftspeople who wanted advice. Recognizing the opportunity to help these people, Emery created Spare Time Promotions.

(Continued on next page)

Biographical Sketch (continued)

From a personal standpoint, Spare Time Promotions was even more fulfilling than jewelry design. On one hand, it helped artists and craftspeople who lacked the skills to market themselves. On the other hand, it enabled Emery and the other artists to support "Young Artists at Risk" —an art program for lower-income children.

By the time Emery graduated from high school, she had established relationships with 15 retail outlets in five communities. She also acted as a marketer/distributor for 30 local artisans. Before she left for college, she recruited and trained four younger students to manage production and distribution.

State University Marketing Club
As a communications major/psychology minor, Emery gained a deeper appreciation for marketing and consumer behavior. During her first semester, she joined the marketing club and was disappointed to see that it lacked focus. Except for an occasional guest lecturer, nothing was ever accomplished.

Seeing the possibility that existed in a group of 15 enthusiastic, would-be marketers, Emery championed a restructuring of the club. After recruiting faculty sponsors from the psychology, communications and economics departments, Emery led a team into the community in search of entrepreneurs and start-up companies. Through this project, she created a win-win situation for the companies and students alike. The companies received free marketing assistance. The club members gained experience writing and presenting marketing plans. Students who participated in more involved projects even received academic credit.

Emery was unanimously elected club president as a sophomore. Within three years of the restructuring, active participation had grown from 15 to 105 students. Graduating members were actively recruited by advertising agencies, start-up companies, and others.

University News/Marketing Column
To ensure ongoing media exposure, Emery convinced the university paper to run a weekly marketing column written by the Marketing Club. The club used the space to promote ongoing and upcoming projects. On occasion, local entrepreneurs wrote special features— usually about their interaction with the Marketing Club. Three months after the column began, club awareness on campus approached 90 percent. Over 75 percent of the new members surveyed pointed to the column as their first exposure to the club.

Other Extracurricular Activities
    Tennis Team: Member (4 years)
    WAVO-FM: Newscaster/Disc Jockey (2 years)
    Special Olympics: Volunteer Coach (6 years)

Note: **The information above is intended as an overview of the fictitious candidate featured in the sample résumés that follow. <u>This is not a résumé.</u>**

THE SKELETON RÉSUMÉ

Emery Stephanie McTell
25 Ocean View Drive
Anytown, USA
(612) 555-1045

EDUCATION   **STATE UNIVERSITY**
B.A. Mass Communications   *(June, 1996)*
Minor/Psychology

RELEVANT   Consumer Behavior   Statistics
COURSES   Creative Writing   Public Speaking
                   Accounting   Economics

RELATED   **STATE UNIVERSITY MARKETING CLUB**
EXPERIENCE   President   *(1994-1996)*
                   - Led weekly meeting
                   - Organized campus activities
                   - Liaison to local businesses and speakers
                   Member   *(1992-Present)*

                   SPARE TIME PROMOTIONS   *(1991-Present)*
                   Sold jewelry and other arts/crafts items to local stores

OTHER   **JUST FOR FUN DESIGNS**   *(1989-Present)*
EXPERIENCE   Started business designing and manufacturing jewelry

ACTIVITIES   **SPECIAL OLYMPICS**   *(1990-Present)*
                   Volunteer Coach
                   UNIVERSITY NEWS
                   Marketing Columnist   *(1992-Present)*
                   WAVO-FM *(Student Radio Station)*   *(1992-Present)*
                   Disc Jockey, Newscaster
                   TENNIS TEAM/*State University*   *(1992-Present)*
                   Member

HONORS &   *1994 Distinguished Young Business Person* (Anytown Chamber of
AWARDS   Commerce), Dean's List, President's Scholarship

COMPUTER   Proficient in Microsoft Word, Harvard Graphics, Charisma, Lotus,
EXPERIENCE   Pro/AR, Adobe Desktop Publishing and QuickBooks.
                   Seasoned Web surfer.

THE CLUTTERED RÉSUMÉ

Emery Stephanie McTell
25 Ocean View Drive
Anytown, USA
(612) 555-1045

EDUCATION

STATE UNIVERSITY
B.A. Mass Communications *(June, 1996)*
Minor/Psychology
Funded over 65% of tuition/spending money through part-time business ventures.

EXPERIENCE

STATE UNIVERSITY MARKETING CLUB
President *(1994-1996)*
Led weekly meetings • Organized campus activities • Secured marketing agreements with local businesses • Designed and monitored work/study programs • Developed business/marketing plans for local entrepreneurs and other small start-up companies • Worked with University to arrange academic credit for special club projects • Booked speakers (e.g., local business owners, advertising executives) • Created campus events to boost club awareness/participation • Represented club to student finance committee • Identified faculty sponsors for the club.

JUST FOR FUN DESIGNS *(1989-Present)*
Designed and manufactured a line of custom jewelry, accessories, and greeting cards • Maintained database of customers for holiday direct mail program • Sold items through local stores • Managed all aspects of the business including accounts receivable, retail support, direct marketing, inventory and sales.

SPARE TIME PROMOTIONS *(1991-Present)*
Represented myself as well as other local artists, entrepreneurs, and craftspeople • Built extensive network of contacts including over 15 local businesses and 30 artisans • Donated portion of proceeds to "Young Artists At Risk" — an art program for lower income children • Recruited and coordinated high school and college students to create awareness and interest in *SPARE TIME* goods • Set prices • Determined profit/loss projections.

ACTIVITIES

***UNIVERSITY NEWS*/Marketing Columnist** *(1992-Present)*
Conceived and wrote a weekly column covering the activities of various student business organizations including the *State University Marketing Club*. Recruited club members and local business owners to appear as guest columnists.

***WAVO-FM* (Student Radio Station)** *(1992-Present)*
Disc Jockey, Newscaster. Hosted Friday evening new music feature. Created Station Promo tapes and Public Service Announcements • Prepared and announced Monday evening news.

***VARSITY TENNIS TEAM*/State University** *(1992-Present)*

HONORS & AWARDS

1994 Distinguished Young Business Person Award (Anytown Chamber of Commerce), voted 1994 Best Columnist/University News, Dean's List (3 years), Presidential Scholarship, 1995 Who's Who in American College Students, Special Olympics Coach (6 years).

COMPUTER EXPERIENCE

Proficient in Microsoft Word, Harvard Graphics, Charisma, Lotus, Pro/AR, Adobe Desktop Publishing and QuickBooks. Seasoned Web surfer.

The distance test

One of the most effective ways to gain insight into the interview's perspective is through the distance test. If you already have written a résumé, use it for this exercise. (Otherwise, photocopy the "skeleton" and "cluttered" résumés that follow the biographical sketch.) Pin the résumés on the wall and stand back five to seven feet. What can you read?

Unless your eyes are exceptionally strong, you will only be able to read the name, the category headings, and possibly a company name or two. What does that say? If it's your résumé, it says that where you worked is more important than what you did. For your sake, I hope that's not true. If you think of the résumé as a one-page ad for you, it makes sense that you wouldn't want the most prominent communication to be "Experience," "Education," and "References available on request."

Content-wise, the skeleton résumé and the cluttered résumé shown on the preceding pages represent opposite extremes. But their similarities are more striking; they are both hopelessly unfocused and sadly typical.

The skeleton résumé

This is a "skeleton" résumé in the sense that it is short on specifics. Without focus and personality, it could literally belong to anyone. The capitalization, the boldface type, the type size, and the white space that surrounds them make the category headings the most prominent elements on the résumé. However, in their existing, generic state, they represent unrealized potential.

In the unlikely event that a recruiter were to spend more than a few seconds reading this résumé, he or she would be struck by the difference between the actual communication and what was probably intended. This issue could be addressed with headings that are both active and skill-focused. "Experience" is neither. Countless people passively experience life. Far fewer make the most of their opportunities.

The fact that Emery chose to subdivide "experience" into "related" and "other" creates further confusion. Theoretically, each point under "related experience" is relevant to the employer. But how? Emery has unintentionally placed the onus on the interviewer to determine how each experience is related. Taking this one step further, "other experience" can only be interpreted as "irrelevant." While this was clearly not intended, the objective remains a mystery. This may have been an attempt to demonstrate other areas of responsibility and achievement. Perhaps she was trying to appear well-rounded. It doesn't matter. Résumés should answer questions, not raise them.

The cluttered résumé

The cluttered résumé may lack focus, but it definitely isn't short on detail. In this case, the detail is so overwhelming that it actually prevents the reader from gaining an appreciation of Emery and her accomplishments. Excessive detail is an interesting problem because it highlights the human tendency to believe that more is better. This, incidentally, is not a belief shared by people who read résumés regularly. A recruiter evaluating this résumé would probably reach the following conclusions:

- Emery doesn't know what I need.

- She doesn't know what she has to offer.

- She doesn't respect my time.

As you weigh the relative merits of your experience, keep in mind that job-hunting is no different than trying out for a team. For example, if you were competing for a spot on the tennis team, the fact that you could swim the 100 yard butterfly in Olympic-qualifying time would be irrelevant. You would have to convince the coach that this skill somehow made you a better tennis player. In much the same way, a résumé cluttered with meaningless detail does not effectively communicate potential.

Perpetrators of Clutter

> Not long after graduation, I received a letter from the college career counselors requesting permission to use my résumé in a collection of well-written résumés. Flattered that anyone considered it impressive, I immediately signed the consent form. Neither the school nor I recognized it as cluttered. I didn't realize the mistake until months later. At that point, I sent a revised résumé with a note explaining why the previous version was ineffective.
>
> This example is not intended as a criticism of guidance counselors in general or mine in particular. It would be unfair to blame anyone else for my own mistake. I am only including it to illustrate that misconceptions exist at all levels of the recruiting process.

Your life on one page

A résumé is not a summary of your experience as dictated by a standard format (i.e., name, objective, education, experience). A résumé is your life, on one page, as it relates to the position you are pursuing. It is also a reflection of the person you are becoming. After reviewing your cover letter and résumé, the reader should be convinced that the position you are pursuing is a logical next step in your development. In this sense, an effective résumé is a synthesis of the insights gained through the self-analysis and target analysis (chapters 1 and 2). A recruiter should be able to glance at the résumé and think:

> "This person knows what I am looking for in an employee.
> There is definite potential here."

What not to include

To make room on the résumé for specific, relevant, and quantified experience, we will first review those facts that can be excluded. This includes:

- objectives/references

- grade point average

Although some recruiters disagree, I feel strongly that this information does not belong on a résumé.

Objectives/References: A clearly stated objective belongs in the cover letter, not the résumé. It isn't necessary or helpful to include flowery, meaningless detail about a "challenging position" at a "progressive company" that "utilizes your organizational skills, attention to detail, and ability to work with people." Sound familiar? I have seen the same objective—stated more or less verbosely—and have never been impressed. If you feel compelled to put an objective on the résumé, keep it simple (e.g., account management, brand management, public relations).

"References available upon request" is another urge you should resist. If you want to clutter your résumé with statements of the obvious, why stop there? Have some fun with it. Here's a few more you might consider:

- Interviews granted by request or appointment

- Salary negotiable

- Will accept promotions/raises

On a more serious note, if your dream job is even somewhat related to sales or marketing and "references available upon request" is your best idea for a final selling message, spare yourself the agony. Find another career.

Grade Point Average (GPA): In the spirit of full disclosure, the GPA and whether it should be included is an area where I differ from many recruiters. For some, GPA is important as an indicator of intelligence, motivation, and the ability to set and achieve goals. Thus, the absence of a GPA raises questions.

I view the GPA differently. If your résumé is focused and truly speaks to the company's needs, the fact that you didn't include a GPA will probably not eliminate you from consideration. Interviewers who are that interested (or narrow-minded) will ask anyway. I, on the other hand, don't care how you were graded or by whom. I want to know what you learned. I want to know whether or not you have the personality, the leadership ability, and the common sense to succeed. I want to know if you will do well on my team. No grade can ever tell me that.

For all but a select few, a stellar GPA represents years of hard work. However, unless you are also applying to medical school, there is no tangible benefit to earning a 4.0. The opportunity cost can be extraordinary. In my office, the extra effort won't earn you any points. Just the opposite. You will have to work harder to convince me that you are active and involved in nonacademic activities. I will also probe deeper than ever on your ability to handle difficult people and uncomfortable situations. If you are truly multidimensional, creative, interesting, and in touch with the world, you won't have trouble convincing me—but we'll waste time getting there.

For comparison, I did not include a GPA on my résumé. Only one inexperienced person ever cared enough to ask. I don't think you need the painful details to imagine how boring the rest of that interview was. While almost no one asked about my grades, a few insightful people did ask what I learned. Life's most valuable lessons are rarely taught in the library.

What to keep short and sweet

Computer Literacy: Within our lifetime, I fully expect that this category will become unnecessary. Until then, its absence raises questions. Unless the company has specific requirements (e.g., extensive Internet experience), cover yourself with: "computer literate."

Preparing the résumé

At this point, forget about writing a résumé and reflect on the topics and questions below. Most of the questions deal with what you have done or hope to accomplish. This information is essential if you hope to market yourself effectively. Nevertheless, the answer to the following question is the key to any successful job search:

"What skills or qualities are important to a particular employer?"

Is it surprising that this has almost nothing to do with you? If, as I suspect, you haven't given this enough attention, don't beat yourself up. Most people don't consider it at all. Not so coincidentally, most people who pursue hard-to-get jobs don't get them either.

Objective

- What is your dream job?

- What attracts you to this career?

- Why would you be good at it?
- What skills or qualities are important to a potential employer?

Education
- Where did you go to school?
- Why did you go there?
- What degree did you earn?
- What classes did you take?
- What classes did you love?
- What did you learn that you can apply to your future career?

Experience
- List all jobs, extracurricular activities, travel, and volunteer experiences.
- What were your job responsibilities?
- Have you ever earned a raise or promotion?
- List any awards you have won.
- Have you ever held an office or other position in a school, church, or volunteer activity? Were you elected or appointed?
- How long were you involved?
- What did you like?
- What didn't you like?
- Why did you get involved?
- List your triumphs over adversity (what, when, how, etc.)

Outside interests/life experiences

- What do you do for enjoyment?

- What makes you unique?

- Have you done or seen anything that most people never experience?

References

- Who, other than family, appreciates and respects your ability?

- Who knows what a competent, hard-working person you are?

- What do people see as your greatest strengths? What would they see as your weaknesses?

Strategic considerations

On a separate sheet of paper, list the required, company-specific skills (e.g., strategic thinking, problem solving, leadership). These will be the focus of both your cover letter and résumé. Using your notes from the questions above, as well as the information from your self-analysis, list the experiences that best demonstrate your ability and potential. Think beyond job titles to actual accomplishments.

Quantifying your experience

Whenever possible, the experiences on your résumé should be results-focused and quantifiable. Consider the difference between the following entries:

General experience:
   Organized fund-raising efforts for the Leukemia Research Foundation (1990).

Quantified/results-oriented experience:
   Created and organized direct-mail fund-raising effort that yielded a record 35 percent participation and an additional $75,000 for bone-marrow transplants (Leukemia Research Foundation, 1990).

The case study on the following page is an excellent example of the power and insight that can come from quantifying personal experience.

CASE STUDY

Concert Violinist Seeks Marketing Position

I was recently approached by a concert violinist who wanted help getting a job in advertising. Not surprisingly, her three-page résumé focused almost exclusively on her experience as a violinist.

I was confused and challenged. First, I had a hard time understanding why a violinist who played with Sir Georg Solti, Daniel Barenboim, and the Moody Blues would make the switch to advertising. Second, assuming her passion for advertising was genuine, how could she possibly position 20 years of orchestral experience to make it clear that account management was the next logical step? How would this transfer to a résumé?

Answers to these questions became apparent only after I challenged her to chart the accomplishments in every area of her life. My questions and instructions were as follows:

- Under what circumstances have you been recognized by others?
- In what areas have you earned additional responsibility?
- How did you get involved in teaching? Did students find you or did you find them?
- How many students have you taught?
- How much did you charge? How have your rates changed?
- Quantify everything.

When she returned with 15 pages of notes, I noticed underlying themes of marketing and leadership in almost every area of her life. Suddenly I understood her interest in account management. She was recognized as a leader at age 12 when she began teaching violin lessons at the music school's request. From there, she marketed herself as a teacher, classroom instructor, musician, and manager of a string quartet. As she described the various marketing challenges, a more focused, enthusiastic person emerged.

We applied this insight to her other experiences with similar results. Even as a temp at a high-end equipment manufacturer, she had established a record of achievement, recognition, and additional responsibility. Examples of strategic thinking and problem solving emerged from each experience. Until that point, every part of her presentation (i.e., cover letter, résumé, interviewing style) positioned her as a concert violinist who suddenly wanted to pursue advertising. Now, her positioning matches her achievements:

She is an accomplished marketer, problem-solver, and strategic thinker who also happens to be a concert violinist.

Outside interests/life experiences

An insightful interviewer can learn a lot from a person's interests and experiences. Assuming that your résumé already speaks to the needs of a particular company, this may be the most important category you include. It might sound strange, but this could ultimately be what distinguishes you from the competition. This category answers four important questions:

- What makes you special?

- Have you had any unique experiences?

- How do you spend your free time?

- What do your outside interests say about the kind of person you are?

Of all the résumés I have seen, my favorite example of this was done by my friend Jerry Dow. His last entry captured his personality in a simple, yet memorable way:

> *A Little Bit More*
> I have also: hauled hay, pumped gas, mixed chemicals, plowed fields, waited tables, worked in a gun shop, worked in a machine shop, worked in the oil fields, photographed birthday parties, tended bar, milked a cow, saved a life, jumped from an airplane, and met Jerry Lewis.

This makes it clear that Jerry values every moment of his life. It is also quite revealing that he would write "milked a cow" and 10 other phrases before "saved a life." It strongly suggests that Jerry is a down-to-earth person who doesn't arrogantly view himself as a hero. Not surprisingly, "A Little Bit More" inspired most of the résumé-related questions that came up in Jerry's interviews. My own résumé includes an entry that was effective for different reasons:

What makes me smile

- teaching preschool

- volunteering (Children's Memorial Medical Center)

- improvisation (Second City/Players' Workshop)

- scuba diving (advanced/rescue)

- skydiving

- CD/record collecting

- stock/options trading

- piano, guitar, trombone, and voice lessons

- poetry

- weight-training

- yoga

At least 80 percent of the questions generated by my résumé came from this category. Without exception, each interviewer wanted to learn more about my involvement in whatever hobby happened to interest them.

When I earned my Open Water Certification for scuba diving, I added it to the list. Of my next four interviews, three were with certified divers. The fourth planned to take classes. How do I know? Before we even sat down, each interviewer asked: "So, where have you been diving?" As fellow divers, we bonded instantly. As an interviewee, there's no better feeling.

Chronological vs. skill-focused

Some recruiters prefer a chronological résumé—particularly for those candidates who already have full-time experience. When the exact chronology isn't apparent, it raises questions:

- Has this person accounted for all of his or her time since college?

- Are there extended periods of unemployment (or underemployment)?

- Has this person made a series of sideways career moves that might indicate a performance or motivation problem?

Your experience—from the perspective of the company's needs—may not be consistent with a chronological presentation. If so, don't leave it up to the interviewer to recreate the sequence of events. Provide a brief time-line in a separate entry.

If there is any significant period of time that you haven't accounted for, address it in the cover letter. As odd as it might seem, this can be a strong selling point. One candidate even used what he learned by failing out of college to demonstrate growth, honesty, and maturity:

For the most part, I led an extremely sheltered, middle class life.

High school was a breeze. My parents expected me to do well and I did. My parents were also strict. I wasn't allowed to drink, stay out late or attend unsupervised parties.

College was my first opportunity to be away from home. I pretty much went bananas. I drank every night. I never studied. I routinely skipped classes. And I wallpapered my room with threats of academic probation. I immaturely viewed college as an $18,000 party paid for by my parents.

I failed out after one year. I could have transferred, but it would have been a Band-Aid solution. Instead, I spent the next few years working and growing up.

From the perspective of an objective observer, this candidate went on to explain what the experience taught him, how he found focus, and his decision to return to pursue a master's degree. When he finished, there was no trace of the designated-drinker who failed out of college. What I saw instead was a determined young man who found wisdom through unconventional means.

Similar companies, different needs

The rest of this section will take the detail of the cluttered résumé and apply it to hypothetical account management positions at Agency A and Agency B. Although both agencies seek energetic, self-starters who possess excellent communication skills (written and verbal), other entry-level requirements differ. The corporate cultures differ as well.

Entry-level requirements/corporate culture

<u>Agency A</u>: Agency A is a conservative agency with conservative clients. Account people who excel in this environment would be described as:

- leaders
- strategic-thinkers
- problem-solvers
- risk-averse
- persuasive

Agency B: This is a younger agency with more progressive clients. To manage the rapidly changing businesses of its clients, Agency B seeks account people who are:

- entrepreneurial
- adventurous
- creative
- intuitive
- resourceful

Respecting personal preferences

The differences between the agencies raise two important questions:

- Can Emery market herself for both positions?
- Should Emery market herself for both positions?

As long as Emery takes the time to position herself appropriately, there is no doubt that she could compete for both. She could probably even excel at either agency. However, her ability to do the work is not a good predictor of long-term professional satisfaction. Emery must know herself well enough to know which environment better suits her personality.

The corporate culture at Agency A might be so rigid that Agency B's top performers would feel stifled. Likewise, Agency A's top performers might be so methodical and process-oriented that they lack the entrepreneurial spirit needed to flourish at Agency B.

To make an informed decision, Emery must be aware of these differences. It may be that Emery is more adventurous than risk averse. Or perhaps she's more creative than strategic. If either is true, she would probably be happier at Agency B. For the same reasons, it would be in Emery's best interest to focus her job search efforts on other creative, entrepreneurial agencies.

When you find yourself weighing the relative merits of different corporate environments, trust your instincts. You may or may not be flexible enough to succeed in different work situations. Just remember, the perfect job is not the one that your parents want you to pursue. And it may not be the one everyone else wants. There is no perfect job—only the one that's best for you.

Tailoring the résumé

For demonstration purposes, let's assume that Emery could be happy in either environment. Given this, how might she position her experience to make it relevant for each agency?

Hint: It would be a mistake for Emery to use the same approach for both agencies.

Consider what would happen if Emery sent both agencies a cover letter and résumé that positioned her as creative, adventurous, and entrepreneurial. At Agency B, this approach could generate interest. At a more conservative agency, it would be meaningless—possibly even detrimental.

The cover letters and résumés on the following pages are approaches that Emery might consider. The first pair is tailored toward Agency A—the conservative corporate agency. The second pair is more appropriate for Agency B. Although the focus differs, the communication is accurate, honest, and relevant.

The conservative agency

To address the needs of Agency A, Emery focuses on leadership, strategic-thinking, persuasiveness, and those aspects of her experience that best support her potential. The cover letter acknowledges these qualities and makes direct comparisons between Emery's developing skills and the requirements of account management. The résumé supports the cover letter with specific, quantifiable accomplishments. Even the headings (Advertising/Marketing, Writing/Presentations Skills) speak to her potential.

The approach described above has another, less obvious benefit. Matching her skills to the company's requirements gives Emery an advantage from an interviewing standpoint. By addressing these basic questions first, the interview can be more focused and productive.

The progressive agency

For Agency B, Emery's challenge is to create a cover letter and résumé featuring the qualities that Agency B seeks in entry-level employees (i.e., entrepreneurial, adventurous, creative, intuitive, and resourceful). The result is a letter that works hard from the first sentence. The unstated message is also clear:

> "I am an adventurous, resourceful person who can navigate her way to interesting opportunities—on and off the Web."

SAMPLE COVER LETTER: *Agency A*
(The conservative company)

Ms. Jennifer Alexander
Agency A
Anytown, USA 99999

Dear Ms. Alexander:

I am writing to express my interest in pursuing a career in account management with AGENCY A. In your presentation at State University last week, you emphasized the Agency's commitment to recruiting persuasive, energetic people who are passionate about marketing. These are just three of the qualities I can offer Agency A.

Over seven years ago, I began designing jewelry as a hobby. Within a few months, I found myself swamped by requests from friends and acquaintances. As demand continued to build, I convinced several local businesses to carry the line under the name Just For Fun Designs.

Before long, I realized that I enjoyed marketing even more than jewelry design. At that point, I shifted my focus and formed Spare Time Promotions. Through this venture, I used my talents to promote local craftspeople. As the liaison between artists and store owners, I operated much like a traditional account executive. I represented the artists to the stores and the stores to the artists in an ongoing effort to manage the needs and expectations of each.

Later, I used the skills that I developed through Spare Time Promotions to lead a team that transformed the Marketing Club at State University. Before the end of the school year, we started working with local businesses on a project basis. As a result, many of these same companies began to recruit at State University.

I would welcome the opportunity to contribute my developing talents to AGENCY A. I will call you in two weeks to set up a meeting at your convenience.

Thank you very much for your time and consideration.

Sincerely,

Emery McTell

SAMPLE RÉSUMÉ: *Agency A*

Emery Stephanie McTell
25 Ocean View Drive
Anytown, USA
(612) 555-1045
e-mail: emctell@state.edu

EDUCATION — **STATE UNIVERSITY** *(June, 1996)*
B.A. Mass Communications; Minor/*Psychology*
Computer Literate

MARKETING — **MARKETING CLUB PRESIDENT** *[Elected for 3 terms]* *(1993-1996)*
STATE UNIVERSITY

Leadership/Team Skills
Became youngest club president (elected unanimously as a sophomore) • Championed club restructuring • Recruited faculty sponsors • Designed club projects with local businesses/entrepreneurs • Represented club to university finance committee

Persuasion/Motivation
Convinced school to award academic credit for club projects/internships • Increased active club membership from 15 to 105 • Attracted 20 new businesses for campus recruiting (12 of these firms then hired 17 seniors over a 2 year period).

FOUNDER/MARKETING REPRESENTATIVE *(1990-Present)*
SPARE TIME PROMOTIONS

Leadership
Represented local artists/craftspeople to area businesses • Generated $2,500.00 per month in sales after 3 years • Recruited, trained and coordinated high school and college students to create awareness and interest in *Spare Time* products.

Strategic Planning
Built extensive network of contacts including over 15 local businesses and 30 artisans • Created customer database • Designed/implemented 3 direct marketing promotions which generated sales increases of 30%, 35% and 45%.

FOUNDER, MARKETER & DESIGNER *(1989-1993)*
JUST FOR FUN DESIGNS

Marketing & Public Relations
Designed/created custom jewelry • Sold items through local stores • Generated awareness/new business by writing feature article on *Just For Fun Designs* that ran in local paper.
Results: Expanded distribution to 3 new retail outlets • 15% sales increase • Five local artists who read the article requested marketing assistance.

WRITING & PRESENTATION SKILLS — **MARKETING COLUMNIST** *(1993 -Present)*
STATE UNIVERSITY NEWSPAPER

NEWSCASTER/DISC JOCKEY *(1993-Present)*
WAVO-FM [Student station]

AWARDS — *1994 Distinguished Young Business Person Award* (Anytown Chamber of Commerce), Dean's List (3 years), Presidential Scholarship

HOBBIES & INTERESTS
Special Olympics Coach (6 years)   Rock climbing
State University Tennis Team (4 years)   Whitewater rafting
Urban impressionist paintings   Rollerhockey
Agatha Christie books   Yoga

CREATING AWARENESS

SAMPLE COVER LETTER: *Agency B*
(The progressive, entrepreneurial company)

Ms. Amber Overholt
Agency B
Anytown, USA 99999

Dear Ms. Overholt:

While surfing on the Internet, I found a link to your Web Page and was truly impressed by what I read. It is refreshing to see an agency so dedicated to entrepreneurial clients that it accepts partial payment in client stock. This vision is what inspires me to explore the possibility of contributing my talents to Agency B.

Over the past seven years, I have experienced the thrill of starting two part-time businesses. In the process, I have begun to develop and nurture many of the qualities that make Agency B successful. Specifically, I have an energetic, entrepreneurial spirit and I am not afraid to take risks. As President of the State University Marketing Club, I was instrumental in nurturing a spirit of teamwork, competition and growth. Aside from the talented young people within the organization, the club's most valuable asset is the sign that hangs prominently on our wall:

> **"Success is not the absence of failure. Rather, it is the ability to view failure as a possible outcome in any worthwhile pursuit. Those who don't fail aren't taking enough chances."**

When I joined the club as a freshman, I was surprised to see 15 enthusiastic members who were not yet committed to the possibility the club represented. From my own experiences in high school, I knew we could gain exposure working as free marketing consultants to local business.

Within a year, we recruited five active faculty sponsors, identified business partners, and convinced the University to award academic credit for more involved projects/internships. As a result, active membership increased 600%.

Like Agency B, the Marketing Club has grown with the companies it serves. In this sense, we have created a partnership between the business leaders of today and tomorrow.

I will call you in two weeks to set up a meeting at your convenience. Thank you in advance for your time and consideration.

Sincerely,

Emery McTell

SAMPLE RÉSUMÉ: Agency B

Emery Stephanie McTell
25 Ocean View Drive
Anytown, USA
(612) 555-1045
e-mail: emctell@state.edu

EDUCATION

STATE UNIVERSITY *(June, 1996)*
B.A. Mass Communications; Minor/Psychology
Computer Literate

MARKETING & ENTREPRENEUR-SHIP

MARKETING CLUB PRESIDENT
STATE UNIVERSITY *(1993-1996)*

Team Skills/Motivation
Championed club restructuring • Recruited faculty sponsors • Designed club projects with local businesses/entrepreneurs • Convinced school to award academic credit for club projects/internships • Increased active club membership from 15 to 105 • Attracted 20 new businesses for campus recruiting (12 of these firms hired 17 seniors in the past 2 years)

FOUNDER
SPARE TIME PROMOTIONS *(1991-Present)*

Initiative
Recognized opportunity to help local artists market their goods/services • Generated $2500.00 per month in sales after 3 years • Self-funded 75% of college tuition/living expenses • Recruited trained and coordinated high school and college students to create awareness and interest in SPARE TIME products

Strategic Planning
Built network of contacts including over 15 local businesses and 30 artisans • Designed/implemented 3 direct marketing promotions which generated sales increases of 30%, 35% and 45%.

CREATIVITY & RESOURCEFULNESS

FOUNDER, JEWELRY DESIGNER
JUST FOR FUN DESIGNS *(1989-1993)*
Designed and created custom jewelry • Generated profit of $200 per week by sophomore year of high school.

MARKETING COLUMNIST
STATE UNIVERSITY NEWSPAPER *(1993 -Present)*
Conceived/wrote weekly marketing feature to gain free publicity for the Marketing Club and upcoming club projects
<u>Results</u> (within 3 Months):
Campus awareness of the restructured Marketing Club exceeded 90% •Of new members surveyed, 75% first exposed to the club through the column.

AWARDS

1994 Distinguished Young Business Person Award (Anytown Chamber of Commerce), Dean's List (3 years), Presidential Scholarship

OUTSIDE INTERESTS

Special Olympics Coach (6 years)   Disc Jockey/Newscaster (Student station)
State U. Tennis Team (4 years)   Agatha Christie books
Whitewater Rafting   Urban Impressionist Paintings
Rock Climbing   Folk Music
Rollerhockey   Yoga

In her approach to Agency B, Emery focuses on her experience as a marketing columnist because of the way she used it as a free publicity vehicle for the Marketing Club. For this reason, it is a great example of resourcefulness. The mileage that Emery gets from this exceeds what she could have achieved using the following experiences (which were not included in this version):

- Marketing Club Rep to the State Univ. Finance Committee
  [leadership]

- Creating customer database for Spare Time Promotions.
  [marketing/strategy]

- Business-generating feature article for Just For Fun Designs.
  [public relations]

The evolving résumé

Creating an effective résumé is an art rather than a science. As such, success is a matter of preparation and persistence. To improve your chances, seek informational interviews. Request feedback. Look for ideas everywhere. You will never have a "final" product. You will evolve and so should your résumé.

Writing Samples

At some point in the recruiting process, you might be asked to submit a writing sample. The topics, which are determined by the company, often relate to personal experiences or industry-specific issues.

> NOT TO TRANSMIT AN EXPERIENCE IS TO BETRAY IT.
>
> —ELIE WIESEL

Life experience

- If you had one day to live over, which one would you choose? Why?

- What is the best advice you have ever received?

- If you could write a letter to your 18-year-old self, what would it say? In other words, what advice or words of encouragement would you give yourself if, at the time of your high school graduation, you could share all that you know now?

What is the company's objective?

It depends on the question and the company. In many cases, a writing sample is used to assess your ability to construct a coherent argument. Depending on the subject, the essay may also provide insights into your personality, values, philosophies, and interests. A great writing sample is important, but it will be useless if you fall flat in the interview.

Expectation vs. reality

I vividly remember one candidate whose essay was truly inspired. In it, he described an entrepreneurial venture directly related to one of my passions. I couldn't wait to meet him. Unfortunately, the vision and inspiration that came through in his essay never surfaced in the interview. Dull, uninspiring, and vanilla are the three kindest words I could use to describe him. I was confused and disappointed. How could anyone write so beautifully and exist so lifelessly?

Later that day, I called another interviewer who met with the candidate to hear his impression. In my heart, I hoped that maybe the candidate and I just didn't click. (In relationships and interviews, chemistry is a curious thing.) As it turned out, the other interviewer shared my disappointment.

As you move through the job search, strive for consistency between your written presentation and the perceptions you create in person. A cover letter or writing sample that sets higher expectations than you can deliver will only work against you.

A WISE MAN KNOWS EVERYTHING: A SHREWD ONE, EVERYBODY.

—UNKNOWN

Building a Network

The only way to impress the right people is to meet them. This may sound basic, but my experience suggests that people are reluctant to seek assistance—particularly when strangers are involved.

Knowing how difficult it is to get a job, I have always done as much as possible to help people in their career search. Although I am listed as an alumni contact for the College of the Holy Cross and Northwestern University, I can count on one hand the number of students who have requested assistance.

Not long after I graduated from Northwestern, some friends and I organized an informational meeting to share what we learned about the recruiting process. About fifty graduate advertising students attended. At the end of the evening, I extended an open invitation to anyone who wanted help in the job search. Secretly, I feared there would be more requests than I could handle.

My fears weren't even partially realized. I received one call the next day and even that person didn't follow through. Several months later, I was surprised to hear that most of the students were still unemployed. As graduation neared, they were shifting into panic mode. The situation described above is sadly typical. The people who worry most about the future are least likely to take steps to shape it.

If the industry professionals I know are any indication, the reluctance to pursue job contacts and informational interviews is widespread. The remedy, however, is simple.

Ask for help before you ask for a job

This is the job hunting equivalent of the "foot-in-the-door" technique used in sales. By honestly seeking the advice of a potential employer, you can get a person to lower his or her defenses.

First, use the career counseling office at your school and an alumni directory to identify contacts. Once you have found several contacts, write a brief note outlining who you are, what you hope to accomplish, and how they can help. If the person is already in the industry, take the time to prepare a résumé that clearly addresses the needs of his or her company.

Finally, request an informational interview and follow up with a phone call. Even if the person doesn't have any helpful ideas, you have lost nothing. On the other hand, he or she may put you in touch with someone at another company or division. It happens all the time.

Avoid human resources

In the information gathering stage, I would advise against contacting alumni who work in human resources—particularly if you want a job at their company. Remember, these people are trained to focus on applicant weaknesses. From a professional standpoint, the biggest mistake a human resources person can make is to recommend an inappropriate candidate. In contrast, when human resources rejects a qualified candidate, it's the company that suffers.

Other networking opportunities

If your parents, friends, and the career counseling office aren't able to help you find contacts, use the techniques described below. If you are resourceful in making contacts, you will have one less quality to demonstrate in an interview.

Trade press/industry experts

Industry-specific magazines (e.g., *Restaurant News*) can be wonderful resources for job hunters. Some even offer regional editions. Find a few that you like and read them faithfully. When you read a relevant or interesting article, contact executives who were quoted. In doing so, make two points clear:

- You value their time.

- You are worthy of their assistance.

One particularly resourceful friend made some of his best contacts by writing to people who had recently been quoted or interviewed. Almost without exception, he received a warm response. People were thrilled to receive the attention. He appealed to their egos and they rewarded him with their time. What more could you want?

The tactic does not have to be limited to job hunting. I have used this technique to secure expert advice on a variety of topics and it hasn't failed yet. Further, I haven't found any correlation between a person's professional or social prominence and their willingness to help. One expert returned my call and spoke for almost 45 minutes. To my surprise, she gave me her schedule as well as her home and work numbers—just in case I had any more questions.

New to the city?

If the job search takes you to an unfamiliar city, contact alumni in the area. The people you call don't even have to be in the same industry. Just send a note and introduce yourself as a recent graduate of their alma mater. Mention that you just moved to the area and ask for ideas, advice, or professional contacts. As always, prepare specific questions.

You might wonder why an alum would take time to help a total stranger who isn't even interested in the same field. It doesn't make sense until you sit on the other side of the desk. That's when it becomes apparent how few candidates are willing to take this step. Nevertheless, it's a risk worth taking because it communicates courage, confidence, and resourcefulness more convincingly than a résumé ever could.

Help wanted ads

In general, job listings are not a good place to find attractive leads. From a purely psychological standpoint, this makes sense. To minimize training and administrative costs–as well as the risk associated with hiring an unknown commodity–a company will often hire from within. When that isn't possible, the company can use word-of-mouth to explore the wider professional community.

Reaching a broader, less-qualified audience through job listings is less efficient. It is also more expensive:

- There is a cost to placing the ad.

- A large response dramatically increases the amount of time that recruiters will have to spend screening unqualified candidates.

Classified ads also have a number of serious shortcomings from the job hunters perspective.

- If the ad is effective, the number of people who respond can be quite high. In other words, interesting positions will attract more applicants.

- The best jobs rarely make the job listings.

Anonymous ads

Responding to an anonymous ad might not seem like an issue, but it is. First, from a purely strategic standpoint, this approach makes almost no sense. How can you position yourself for a job and a company you know nothing about? Don't waste your time.

This risk is substantially higher for people who are currently employed because their own company may have placed the ad. This little faux pas would have the same impact on a person's job security as sending the boss an e-mail that read:

> "My heart's not in it right now. If you can't reach me, I'm probably out looking for work."

CASE STUDY

The Hard Work of Being in the Right Place at the Right Time

Jim Floyd—a Philadelphia-based publicity consultant—is one of those rare individuals who seems to have found the perfect career. Anyone meeting him for the first time would be impressed by his peaceful, easygoing nature. Among his many gifts is the ability to form genuine bonds with friends and strangers alike. However, what makes Jim even more exceptional is what he went through to become the person he is today. Jim endured more than a few disappointments before achieving a sense of personal and professional satisfaction.

Dreams, delight, and disappointment
As his high school classmates wrote college applications, Jim found himself thinking more about singing, acting, and a career on the stage. Although Jim's family respected his talents, they were deeply concerned when he decided to skip college. In his parents' opinion, Jim wasn't taking a risk, he was making a mistake. They didn't see how his passion or ability could overcome a lack of experience, an absence of formal training, or the intense competition. Fortunately, Jim trusted his instincts and focused on his goal.

After graduation, Jim put his heart and voice into auditions. Through persistence, he earned the lead role in a production that eventually toured the country. For the next few years, life was better than he ever imagined.

During his third season with the touring company, Jim lost his voice in the middle of a performance. Unable to speak and deeply concerned, Jim sought the help of a throat specialist. A thorough examination confirmed the worst. Jim's vocal chords showed signs of prolonged strain and abuse. His speaking voice would eventually return, but the damage was permanent. He would never sing again. His career was over.

Knowing that the condition was preventable made the circumstances even harder to accept. Had Jim taken voice lessons, he could have acquired the skills that would have preserved his career. Unfortunately, the natural power and character of his voice camouflaged the underlying need for instruction.

Preparing for Opportunity
With little more than a high school education and a vague desire to remain in the entertainment industry, Jim began his search for a new career. Jim faced another unexpected obstacle when family considerations made it necessary to return to Pennsylvania. Despite this new constraint, his spirit remained intact.

(Continued on next page)

CASE STUDY (continued)

Because Pennsylvania wasn't exactly the entertainment center of the universe, Jim knew he might have to commute as far as New York or New Jersey. Though far from ideal, this was a sacrifice Jim was willing to make to help his family through a difficult time.

Before leaving his Nashville home, Jim contacted a headhunter and explained his situation. To Jim's surprise, the headhunter had just read an interesting but unqualified lead in the classified section of the newspaper. A publication identified only as *"Radio/TV Interview Reports"* was conducting a nationwide search for someone to act as a liaison between television producers and talk show guests. Interested applicants were given the following instructions:

> *We don't care about your résumé. We are more interested in how you come across on the phone. Call the toll-free number. Leave a message. Tell us why we should hire you. If we like what we hear, we'll call you back.*

For Jim, this wasn't enough. He picked up the phone, but he didn't call the 800 number. Instead, he called directory assistance to find out who owned the number. The phone company wouldn't reveal the customer's name, but it did tell him where the calls were directed. To his delight, the town was in Pennsylvania. With the help of a local phone book, Jim compiled a list of six companies that could have placed the ad. A few phone calls later, Jim had narrowed his search to one company—Bradley Communications. But his homework was not finished. By learning more about the company and its publication, Jim gained a better appreciation of the requirements of the position. Once Jim knew which skills to highlight, he sent a letter directly to the company's president.

By the end of the search, Bradley Communications had heard from 1,200 interested applicants. Although many offered more in the way of education and experience, none could match Jim for enthusiasm, perseverance, and potential. Jim was the only person who took the time to identify the company and understand its business. Not surprisingly, he got the job.

Career Update
As publicity liaison for *Radio/TV Interview Reports*, Jim worked hard to build and strengthen partnerships with producers and talk show guests alike. Over time, Jim developed a reputation as a trusted and effective advocate for his clients. This gave Jim the courage to take the next step in his professional evolution—self-employment.

> *THE STRENGTH OF A MAN'S VIRTUE SHOULD NOT BE MEASURED BY HIS SPECIAL EXERTIONS, BUT BY HIS HABITUAL ACTS.*
>
> —PASCAL

Correspondence

My thoughts on the importance of written and verbal correspondence can be summed up in one sentence:

Be polite and professional in every encounter with a company, its employees, and its clients.

This includes contact with secretaries, receptionists, mail-carriers—everyone! Leave anyone you meet with a smile.

Letters

Treat every cover letter, résumé, writing sample, and thank you note as an example of your professionalism and writing ability. If you struggle as a writer, take a class. Without it, your chances of being hired by a competitive company are substantially reduced.

Thank you notes

So few people take the time to write follow-up notes (of any kind) that they convey a powerful, positive message out of proportion to the effort. Thank you notes are particularly important after an interview. It won't impact the company's decision. Rather, it's common courtesy—which tragically isn't all that common. Thank you notes arrive in one of two forms: business letters or greeting cards. When in doubt, the business letter format is a safe option.

If you have multiple interviews on the same day, send a separate note to everyone who interviewed you—and anyone else who went out of their way to help. A single note to the company is not enough. The letters shouldn't be long. However, you should include a specific reference to your conversation to help you reconnect with the interviewer. This will be easier if you take notes after each interview. Otherwise, a full day of interviews will be one big blur.

Phone calls

If you tell somebody you will call on Tuesday, call Tuesday. Leave a message if necessary. Otherwise, you may be perceived as unreliable. I was fortunate to learn this lesson through someone else's mistake. As I sat in the General Manager's office at WUSN-FM (US99) in Chicago, a voice came over the intercom: "Steve, Brad—on line two— is inquiring about the position, will you take the call?" Without blinking, Steve replied:

> "No. He was supposed to call yesterday. Please tell him we have nothing for him."

That was it. Steve wasn't interested in explanations. Neither are clients. Call when you say you will call.

Sending gifts . . . lessons from the circular file

Some people are overcome by the urge to buy trinkets and gifts for interviewers. My advice on this is simple—don't. Once the interview is over, nothing you can do will positively impact the outcome. A gift will only ensure that you are remembered for the wrong reasons.

Not long after one interview, I received a hand-delivered thank you note and a pair of Nike athletic socks. According to the note, I was supposed to remember the socks when I asked myself whether or not we should hire this person. Of course, I was instructed to "Just do it!"

Perhaps the use of a famous advertising slogan was supposed to impress me. Who knows? Even beyond the bizarre premise and execution, I was mystified by the ignorance. Why would anyone send Nike socks to a company that represented Reebok? Ouch!

PART 2

Making the Sale

Consumer Perceptions

Direct Selling: *The interview*

Improving Your Technique and Closing the Deal

Make visible what, without you, might perhaps never be seen.

—ROBERT BRESSON

CHAPTER 4

Consumer Perceptions

Videotaped Mock Interviews

One of the most valuable services offered by career counseling professionals is the videotaped mock interview. If videotaping isn't an option (and it should be), a regular mock interview is still an excellent idea. Either way, this opportunity for practice and constructive criticism can enhance your performance.

Video is particularly effective because it provides a level of objectivity and insight otherwise impossible to achieve. Watching yourself on tape will give you a deeper appreciation of the perceptions you create. You may even be surprised by nervous habits that operate beyond your conscious awareness.

To maximize the benefits of a mock interview, prepare as if it were an actual interview. Ask the interviewer to represent a specific company. (Having done your homework, you know some of the questions to expect.) After the videotaped session, review the tape twice. First, scan through the tape and listen to the other person's insights. Then, watch the entire interview and answer the following questions:

- How concisely did I respond?

- How well did I communicate my strengths?

- Did I smile?

- How might I appear more poised, confident, and convincing?

If you make it through the entire tape without beating yourself to death, take a few days to reflect on the experience. Then, tape another interview. Success takes practice.

MOST IGNORANCE IS VINCIBLE IGNORANCE. WE DON'T KNOW BECAUSE WE DON'T WANT TO KNOW.

—ALDOUS HUXLEY

AN EXPERT IS SOMEONE WHO KNOWS SOME OF THE WORST MISTAKES THAT CAN BE MADE IN HIS SUBJECT AND HOW TO AVOID THEM.

—WERNER HEISENBERG

Informational Interviews

The primary objective of an informational interview is to gather knowledge not available from a published source. It is not a substitute for library research.

Anyone who grants an informational interview does so with the expectation that he or she will not be put on the spot for a job. Don't violate this trust. Although you won't be asking for a job, you will still be evaluated. Treat it as a formal interview and act accordingly. As the person who requested the meeting, it is your responsibility to guide the conversation. You should have two primary objectives:

- to learn as much as possible about a company or industry.
- to explore ways to market yourself more effectively.

Depending on the person's position/title, you may have to use different approaches. This shouldn't matter, but it often does.

Chief Executives

If you are fortunate enough to line up an interview with a CEO or top-ranking officer of a company, congratulations—you have earned a wonderful opportunity. But be ready. These can be the toughest people to impress. Unlike people in middle and lower management, CEOs are often bombarded by friends and acquaintances acting on behalf of their children.

To complicate matters further, CEOs also have a different recruiting perspective. A CEO isn't motivated by the financial incentives or corporate recognition that mid-level managers often receive for recruiting top candidates. For these reasons, you need a slightly different strategy.

The lecture

CEOs are the only executives I have encountered who will grant an informational interview not to answer questions, but to deliver a canned lecture on the "very specific needs" of their company. With this agenda in mind, not one executive ever stopped to find out whether or not I had any relevant experience. They assumed that I did not.

My first meeting with a person in upper management took place during my senior year in college. After listening patiently to the COO (Chief Operating Officer) describe how his agency never hires people right out of college, I knew I needed a new strategy—fast. Inspired, I said:

"Well, perhaps you can help me in a different way. I have an interview tomorrow with an executive vice president at Foote, Cone & Belding. Could you take a quick look at my résumé and tell me what I might do to improve the way I am marketing myself?"

Realizing that he wasn't on the spot to give me a job, he relaxed completely and looked over my résumé. Fortunately, my résumé communicated my accomplishments and qualifications in a way that captured his interest. Suddenly, I was exactly where I wanted to be—selling myself in a two-way conversation. He even gave me a few helpful tips. Not two hours later, a senior vice president from the same company called me at home. The COO had given him my name. The agency that "didn't hire people right out of college" suddenly wanted me to come in for an interview.

Answers without questions

For the scenario described above to work, you must interview the interviewer. This is a four-step process:

- Ask questions that encourage the interviewer to reveal how they evaluate candidates.

- Rephrase the answers as a questions.

- Answer the questions as if you were in an interview.

- Ask for feedback.

Here's how the dialogue might occur:

> CANDIDATE: "What do people in your position look for in an entry-level applicant?" (Note: This question is more objective and less personal than "What do you look for. . .?")

> INTERVIEWER: "Three things. X, Y, and Z."

> CANDIDATE: "So, you want to know X, Y, and Z? To convince an interviewer that I have potential in those areas, I would probably discuss experiences A, B, and C. Experience A demonstrates X because. . ., B demonstrates Y because. . ., and C demonstrates Z because . . . (pause). Is this an effective approach? How might I be more convincing?"

THE 20-SECOND TELEPHONE INTERVIEW

As I prepared to make the switch from advertising to options trading, I called the Executive Vice President of an options firm to set up an informational interview. Having just started to identify my alternatives, I had two objectives:

- To get feedback on my strategy (i.e., repositioning myself from advertising to trading).

- To ask about other job opportunities within the industry.

Unrealistic expectations
Since I was given the EVP's name by one of his wife's best friends, it never occurred to me that he might not agree to meet. But that's what almost happened. Rather than set up a time, he said abruptly:

> "Call me in 45 minutes after the market closes. Then, I'll have a minute to see if a meeting is even warranted."

I knew immediately that this was a person who was fiercely protective of his time. Therefore, I would only have a few sentences to convince him I was worth talking to. For the next half hour, I outlined the key points I wanted to communicate. When I called back 45 minutes later, the conversation went something like this:

> "My grandfather, who was a soybean trader at the Board of Trade, sparked my interest in trading and investing when he helped me buy my first stocks at age 10. It's been my passion ever since.
>
> Although I have enjoyed my career in advertising, I've decided to become a floor trader at an exchange. More than anything, I don't want to stay put, reach the end of my life and wonder how things might have been different had I taken the chance."

With that, I heard him take a deep breath. After a pause he said the words I most wanted to hear:

> "We really should meet. Can you come by tomorrow at 3:30?"

The informational interview
The next day, I started the conversation by telling him how much I appreciated his time and what I hoped to accomplish. We proceeded to talk at length about opportunities in the industry. Afterwards, he gave me a few hypothetical trading scenarios and asked about my strategy for each. At that point, he launched into a description of the firm's training program and its advantages over the rest of the industry. He closed by saying:

> "We don't have any openings right now. But if you're interested, call me in two months. We should have something then."

In the interim, I continued to do informational interviews and industry research. Following the EVP's advice, I called him two months later. Fortunately, his company had an opening and I took it.

In effect, this line of questioning leads the person through their own interview—answers first. Because this is an informational interview, you can practice your own answers in a trial and error format. This provides access to instant feedback, constructive criticism, and coaching. Depending on how helpful the other person is, you may reach the end of the interview and find that he or she is sold on your potential. You might even have a job.

Human resources

With certain exceptions, I have found interviews with human resources people to be fruitless. Not once have I ever made it past the initial screening. In contrast, I have been invited back for additional interviews almost every time I talked with someone from a specific department.

Whenever possible, talk to the people with whom you will be working. This makes sense because you need to evaluate them as much as they need to evaluate you. Furthermore, you cannot possibly get all of your questions answered by someone who has never worked in the field.

The follow-up

The only difference between informational and formal interviews is in the follow-up. At the end of an informational interview, ask for the names of people you might contact at other companies. Then, set the expectations for a continuing dialogue:

> "Would you mind if I called next month to see if you've heard any interesting leads?"

You won't be perceived as a desperate pest if the person honors your request and expects your call. Keeping in touch is also a good way to remain top-of-mind with your contacts. These people may be too busy to call you when they hear about opportunities. It might not even occur to them. However, if you are persistent, there is a good chance that people will remember you at the right time for the right reason.

ON FASHION:
IT DOESN'T HAVE TO MATCH. IT JUST HAS TO GO.

—UNKNOWN

Dressing Appropriately

Much has already been written about dressing for interviews, so I won't rehash it here. Whether you are a man or a woman, the bottom line is this: wear a suit—any suit. You can express yourself and have a little flair, just make sure you look professional.

The blue suit myth

When I was preparing for interviews with Leo Burnett, career counselors reminded me again and again that Burnett was a "conservative Midwestern agency where everybody wears a blue pin-striped suit." Before long, they had me convinced that I would have to "look the part." Perhaps that's why I hate blue suits to this day. My time would have been better spent learning to relax.

As it turned out, the fashion insight wasn't accurate anyway. Advertising professionals wear every style and color you can imagine. Very rarely did I even wear a suit at Leo Burnett. As I write this, more and more businesses are adopting casual dress codes. Regardless, job applicants should still wear a suit because it conveys respect for the interviewer. It also shows that you have the good sense to dress professionally for important meetings.

CHAPTER 5

Direct Selling
The Interview

The purpose of this chapter is to present a clear picture of the interview process. This includes an in-depth examination of my own interviewing methods as well as other styles you might encounter. As an interviewee, you have the right to know what is expected. At the same time, it is important to recognize that there is more than one way for interviewers to accomplish their objectives. I neither want, nor expect, agreement from the corporate community on this subject. To achieve consensus is to accomplish nothing.

Given the complexity of the interviewing process, this chapter will be the most comprehensive. It is also potentially the most valuable. If a book like this had been available a few years ago, my own interviewing process would not have been the long, demanding experience that it was.

> *IDEAL CONVERSATION MUST BE AN EXCHANGE OF THOUGHT, AND NOT, AS MANY OF THOSE WHO WORRY MOST ABOUT THEIR SHORTCOMINGS BELIEVE, AN ELOQUENT EXHIBITION OF WIT OR ORATORY.*
>
> —EMILY POST

> *MEN SHOULD BE WHAT THEY SEEM.*
>
> —SHAKESPEARE

What is an Interview?

An interview is a two-way conversation intended to help a candidate and an employer assess mutual fit. As self-explanatory as this might seem, it is precisely the two-way nature of this communication that people forget. This is particularly true of recent college grads who feel anxious about the job search and self-conscious about their lack of experience.

No experience? Great! When can you start?

Entry-level candidates shouldn't spend any time or energy apologizing for their lack of experience—especially in an interview. The assumption that potential employers will react negatively to the absence of full-time experience is both false and dangerous. Any company that interviews recent college graduates is fully aware that experience will be limited or nonexistent. Anyone with experience wouldn't be interviewing for an entry-level position.

Measuring potential

For the most part, the specific needs of a company will dictate the way it assesses potential. Listed below are eight broad categories that can apply to any profession. Use this list as a starting point as you match your skills with the needs of a particular company.

- interpersonal skills
- analytical ability
- writing ability
- problem solving skills
- personality
- communication skills
- idea generation
- adaptability

The challenge, for applicant and interviewer alike, is to cover each category in a 45-minute interview. To accomplish this, and still leave time for the candidate's questions, is even more difficult. On the other hand, it would be even more difficult if you didn't realize the evaluation covered so many areas. Getting hired would take a miracle. In reality, this is precisely how companies rely on applicants to eliminate themselves. The selection process is rigorous, but one way or another, the applicants make it easier.

Making Sense of a Flawed Process

On a practical level, one of the only differences between a job offer and a marriage proposal is the purpose of the relationship. Whether the agreement is to create babies, ideas, or widgets, the relationship requires time, effort, commitment, communication, patience, and understanding.

It hardly makes sense that two people could comfortably enter into a serious relationship after spending a full day or less together. Yet, it happens in the job market every day.

> *Nothing so much prevents our being natural as the desire to seem so.*
>
> —*La Rochefoucauld*
>
> *It ain't braggin' if you kin do it.*
>
> —*Dizzy Dean*

An interviewer's dilemma

I never thought much about the nature of the recruiting process until I became an interviewer myself. Only then did I ask the questions that eventually defined my philosophy:

- How might interviewing be different if we entered jobs the way we enter marriages?

- If I had only 45-minutes to meet and interact with a woman before we decided whether or not to get married, what could each of us do to make a more informed decision?

- What would I want to know about her?

- What would she want to know about me?

- Do I know myself well enough to provide an accurate picture of my goals, strengths, weaknesses, interests, idiosyncrasies, and preferences?

- Do I listen well enough to understand and appreciate who she is as a person?

My approach

As an interviewer, my goal is to minimize the risks associated with entering into a professional relationship. The following questions guide my evaluation:

- Can this person excel in the position?

- Will he or she add value to the team?

- How does this person think?

- How might this person behave in stressful or difficult situations?

- Does this person have the confidence and maturity to express a different point of view without being disagreeable?

My goal is to evaluate the candidate's potential in the context of a relaxed, yet challenging conversation. Since the interview is a two-way exchange, I also provide honest answers to any and all questions. I expect the same in return.

The first moments of an interview

After meeting and shaking hands, there may be a few minutes of casual conversation that can be initiated by either person. For example, the applicant might express an interest in a picture on my office wall. Likewise, I might want to know more about a personal interest listed on the person's résumé. Whatever this case, this brief exchange allows us to absorb our surroundings and establish common ground. It is also important because it can begin to reveal the person's level of enthusiasm and passion for life.

The opening statement

To create a relative level of comfort and to ensure that the candidate focuses on my questions, I say:

> "With luck, I will be asking questions you have never been asked. At times, it might seem like you will never get to tell me about your interesting, career-related experiences. Don't worry. We will have time toward the end for you to tell me anything and everything I should know. At that point, you can ask me any questions at all. If you ask it, I'll answer it. That includes questions about the interview itself, and why I ask what I ask."

This minimizes the chance that the person will become preoccupied and nervous when he or she realizes that I haven't asked specific questions about their internship, college courses, or experiences abroad.

Before you read any further, review the outline of my interview on the next page and answer these questions:

- What is each question meant to assess?

- How would you respond?

- What do your answers reveal about the thoroughness of your preparation?

INTERVIEW TOPICS AND QUESTIONS

- How would you most like to be remembered?
- What other career opportunities are you exploring?
- If you could do anything (career-wise) and money wasn't an issue, what would you do?
- If you could take any classes—without regard to credits, majors, or other academic requirements—what would you study?
- What is one of the best ideas you have ever had?
- If you could invent anything, what would it be?
- You have just written your autobiography. What is on page 73?
- What is the most difficult situation you have ever encountered in dealing with people? How did you address it?
- Give me an example of problem solving.
- Give me an example of resourcefulness.
- What are some of your personal interests?
- Creative Assessment Exercise (Using specific ads)
- Why do you want to work in this field?
- Why do you want to work here?
- Other than our founder, what famous person—real or fictional—best represents our corporate culture? Why?
- The Adjective Questions
  (These are asked, in order, about 20 minutes into the interview.)

  - What are five adjectives your best friend would use to describe you?

  - Someone who doesn't know you well doesn't like you. What are five adjectives he or she might use to describe you?

  - What are five adjectives I might use to describe you?

  - You've known me now for about 25 minutes. What are five adjectives you might use to describe me?

- Is there anything else I should know?
- Do you have any questions for me?

What I like to see

For the most part, I don't ask questions in any particular order. Some issues need to be probed in greater detail, so I improvise. Like any good conversation, an interview requires flexibility and "give and take" by each party. For this reason, I strive to guide rather than control. People who do well in my interviews have at least four characteristics in common:

- They have conducted a thorough personal assessment.

- They are honest about their strengths and weaknesses.

- They understand the qualities that are essential for the position.

- They ask insightful questions.

People who struggle in my interviews haven't thought enough about who they are and what they hope to accomplish. I don't expect people to be fortune tellers, but I do expect to hear compelling testimony about the choices they have made and the lessons they have learned.

I never ask nebulous, meaningless questions like: "Where do you see yourself in five years? 10 years? 15 years?" An insightful, motivated person will evaluate circumstances and opportunities as they develop. There is absolutely no way to know where any of us will be in five years. Nor is it important. There are better ways to assess interest, motivation, and commitment than by asking essentially factual questions about career paths.

The questions behind the questions

"How would you most like to be remembered?"

Your response should include detail and reasoning. What is important to you? What are your personal goals? This is another way of asking:

> "How might you live your life so that if your 60-year-old self were to meet your 20-year-old self, they could look each other in the eye, greet each other warmly, and know that they lived admirably and with no regrets?"

Because this question deals with personal values, it is not one you should answer in relation to a particular career. It would be a mistake to say that you, as a budding marketing executive, want to be remembered as the person who successfully repositioned Screaming Yellow Zonkers. This not only misses the point, but also risks being a brief and entirely meaningless legacy.

It is also best to avoid any response that leaves the interpretation to me. For example, it isn't enough to say, "I want to be remembered as a nice person." Nice could imply that you are a thoughtful, kind person who strives to treat humans and animals with respect. Nice is also a totally innocuous word used to describe people (e.g., blind dates) who lack exceptional intellectual or physical qualities. If your goal really is to be remembered as "nice," convince me that you are living the way you want to be remembered:

- What have you done to realize this goal?

- What have you done that isn't consistent with this objective? Given the chance to relive those moments, what would you do differently?

- What are the biggest obstacles you face? How do you handle them?

"What other career opportunities are you exploring?"

There is nothing wrong with having other career options. What makes most people interesting is a variety of passions. As a bright, educated person, you have probably considered other options. Be honest about the relative merits of each. After all, you have done your homework and have valid reasons for pursuing a particular area of interest. Be persuasive and specific.

To say that the career for which you are interviewing is the only one you have considered will only raise the obvious question: "What will you do if these companies reject you?"

"If you could do anything (career-wise) and money wasn't an issue, what would you do?"

Even if you never hear this question in an interview, it is one you should ask yourself from time to time. You may be amazed how your answer changes over time. This is a particularly good question to ask yourself at the beginning of your career search, and again if you change careers. Never dismiss your talents and interests by saying: "I could never make money doing that." It may help to consult one of the many books that have been written about living your dreams (e.g., *Do What You Love and the Money Will Follow*, by Marsha Sinetar).

"If you could take any classes—without regard to credits, majors, or other academic requirements—what would you study?"

This question is interesting because of the responses it elicits. Too often, candidates use it as an opportunity to apologize for the fact that they don't have an MBA or other advanced degree. This is the wrong answer. Consider the difference between a positive answer and an apologetic one:

Candidate 1: "What a great opportunity! I have always wanted to take a course in photography. I have some natural talent for composition, but I have never had any formal photographic training. I'd also love to take a few courses in music and art appreciation."

Candidate 2: "I have thought about getting an MBA. I probably still will at some point. From what I understand, many of my future clients and co-workers already have the degree. It would be nice to speak to them in the same language. If I can't get a job, that's probably what I'll do."

Each response reveals something different. Candidate 1 views education and learning as an end in itself—a way to better appreciate the world. In contrast, Candidate 2 is preoccupied with the fact that he or she does not have an MBA. To this person, education is strictly a means to an end. Candidate 2 does not appear to have any natural intellectual curiosity—just a warped sense of what he or she thinks I want to hear. Clearly, Candidate 1 scores higher for confidence, enthusiasm, maturity, and motivation.

"What is one of the best ideas you have ever had?"

This question is to your career what a "gimme putt" is to golf. It should take almost no thought and very little effort. At some point, you should have had a few ideas. I don't want to hear all of them, just one. Your creative solutions to problems and your ability to identify opportunities should be among the strengths that you uncovered in your self-assessment. This is your chance to talk about it.

I mentally deduct points for people who look up with surprise and say, "That's a good question. Let me think about it for a second." You shouldn't have to. However, I do remember one impressive exception. The woman sat upright, smiled gleefully and exclaimed, "I've had so many! Let me think about which one was best." I knew instantly that she would be spending a quiet moment weighing the relative merits of a wide range of ideas—not grasping for cosmic enlightenment.

This is probably my favorite question because of the way people react to it. Uninhibited candidates—who are truly passionate about ideas—get a visible adrenaline rush and a wild look in their eyes. Their less enthusiastic counterparts usually have the same expression you see when people describe the classic stress nightmare that wakes people up wondering whether or not they actually graduated from high school.

Unfortunately, most of the memorable responses were proprietary so I can't reveal them. My favorite non-proprietary idea came from the future marketing executive who described her dream of building a house with two dishwashers—so she would never have to unload!

"If you could invent anything, what would it be?"

In many respects, this is similar to the previous question, only more specific. The unspoken question is:

> "What product or service have you identified that would greatly simplify your life or that of someone else?"

At first glance, this question might seem advertising-specific. It isn't. What I like about this question is the way it measures potential in the areas of problem-solving and idea-generation. In this sense, some level of creative thinking applies to any challenging human pursuit (e.g., architecture, genetic engineering, electrical engineering).

As you prepare your response, remember that the question doesn't ask for a solution. Rather, it asks you to identify an unmet need. If you have a specific solution in mind, great. But you don't have to.

If I could invent anything, I would invent a tool for peeling pomegranates. Although it's one of my favorite fruits, I rarely eat more than one or two per year. Peeling the leathery skin and separating the seeds from the inner shell is just too time consuming and messy. Or maybe I'm too lazy. It doesn't matter. That's the opportunity I see.

You might be wondering why I used the example above to illustrate an unmet need. You're right to wonder. "Need" is a fairly strong word to use in reference to a pomegranate. I just wanted to point out that the question doesn't beg for a "save the world" idea. It's appropriate—even advisable—to have a memorable or off-the-wall response. Necessity may be the mother of invention, but that doesn't mean that laziness, convenience, and fun are never its fathers.

"You've just written your autobiography. What is on page 73?"

This is strictly a fun question that probes your ability to think creatively and spontaneously. You could also use this opportunity to reveal an interesting fact about yourself that would otherwise be irrelevant.

"What is the most difficult situation you have ever encountered in dealing with people and how did you address it?"

This can be a decisive question. To be successful in any career, you must work well with a wide range of personalities and temperaments. At times, you will find yourself in situations that require immediate, corrective action to maintain peace and keep everyone focused on common goals. Not surprisingly, this requires superior listening skills, communication skills, honesty, and leadership.

If necessary, take a quiet moment to structure your answer. Briefly outline the conflict, the alternatives, the solution, and the outcome. Say what you learned, why it was a good experience, and how you might handle it more effectively if you had it to do over.

I will never forget one determined interviewee who described in great detail how he might "collect information" about the person who "didn't like him." It was clear that he would talk to anyone other than the person with whom he had the conflict. I wasn't impressed.

One of the keys to resolving work-related disagreements is to stay focused on shared professional objectives. I'll never forget how struck I was the first time I saw two executives in a heated discussion. When they resolved the dispute, they shook hands. With a quick smile, one said, "It's always business, never personal." Unlike some arguments, I was not left with the sense of lingering emotions or unresolved issues. All that remained was a memory of the smile, the handshake, and the profound respect they shared for each other.

No one will ever ask you to love all of your clients, co-workers, and business associates. You don't even have to like them. But if you have to work together, it is critical that you maintain trust and respect, stay focused on the objectives, and address problems openly. To get along with people, I've found it helpful to remember my parents' advice: "Be genuinely interested in others. You can like anybody if you try."

"Give me an example of problem-solving."

This is as straightforward as it gets. Give me evidence that you recognize and address problems effectively. This doesn't have to be work-related. A roommate conflict, a dispute over an insurance claim, and other personal examples are equally valid. It's a good idea to have as many as 10 examples ready. This can include situations that you would handle differently given the opportunity. Discussing an alternative approach also shows that you recognize opportunities for self-improvement.

One interviewer grilled me on this question almost exclusively. By the end of the interview, I had been asked for eight examples of my problem-solving ability.

"Give me a personal example of resourcefulness."

Tight deadlines, last-minute requests, and unforeseen complications demand a high level of resourcefulness and problem-solving from everyone who works as part of a team. Any experience in these areas can be a great predictor of your success on the job.

The nature of this question demands that you know yourself well enough to freely discuss this ability. Here again, have several examples in mind. This isn't the kind of thinking you'll want to do as the sweat drips down your forehead in an interview.

"What are some of your personal interests?"

If you already have this category on the résumé, I will inquire about a specific interest. For each, be prepared to give a brief background:

- How long have you been involved?

- Have you ever been recognized for achievement in this area?

- What do you cherish most about your involvement?

A good answer not only demonstrates enthusiasm, sincerity, and commitment but also convinces me that you are a relatively interesting person who can interact well with clients, co-workers, and business associates.

Creative Assessment

Even though this exercise is advertising-specific, I am including it as an example to clarify the basic concepts of marketing communication. The same principles apply to people who market themselves.

The exercise itself is straightforward. After I show the candidate several magazine ads or television commercials, I ask these questions:

- Is it good or bad advertising?
    - If it's bad, what could be done to improve it?
    - If it's good, what is good about it?

- Who is the target?

- How is the product positioned?

- What is the product benefit?

This exercise measures critical thinking and persuasiveness. To do well, you must demonstrate an understanding of a few basic marketing concepts:

- positioning
- product benefits
- product attributes

Positioning refers to the nature of the product—what it is, who needs it, and how it's different from similar products. The benefit is the way in which the product improves or simplifies a consumer's life. Don't confuse this with the product attributes from which benefits often arise.

THE DISTINCTION BETWEEN ATTRIBUTES AND BENEFITS

> The Interplak Electric Toothbrush
> The fact that the bristles rotate is an attribute, not a benefit. The benefit is the cleaner mouth and fresher breath that presumably result from more effective brushing. Fewer cavities and lower dental bills are also benefits. A good product can have several benefits. Good advertising focuses on one.

"Why are you interested in this career? (e.g., "Why advertising?")

For discussion purposes, let's pretend that you are applying for an advertising job. In this case, you should focus on the challenges and opportunities that intrigue you. For example:

- convincing current users of a product to use more.

- repositioning a product to appeal to a different audience.

- new product introductions.

To be even more convincing, use this opportunity to mention that you have skills that match the employer's needs. For example, you are:

- a critical thinker

- a problem-solver

- a good negotiator

- an effective communicator

- a good motivator

Whatever you do, don't give the classic couch spud answer:

> "Well, I have always loved working with people. I watched a lot of television as a child. For as long as I can remember, I have been more interested in the commercials than in the television programs. I also consider myself very creative. I'm constantly drawing."

So many people get this question wrong that I've learned not to ask it until the end of the interview. It's just too depressing to ask it first and discover that I'm about to waste my next hour. It also becomes too tempting to interrupt the interview for what promises to be the person's final tour of the company.

"Why do you want to work here?"

This should be approached as three separate questions:

- "How much do you know about the company?"
- "Why would you thrive here?"
- "What do you have to offer?"

If you focus exclusively on the company's reputation without regard to what you have to offer, you may create the impression that you see the job as a springboard to better opportunities. This may be true, but don't say it. The company is much more focused on using you and paying but a stipend for the privilege.

"Other than our founder, what famous person—real or fictional—best represents our corporate culture? Why?"

Every company, large and small, has its own unique principles that shape employee behavior. What are these principles or philosophies? Are they written as formal operating procedures or simply understood? How would you personify this aspect of the corporate environment? If no single person fits the image, consider a combination.

A strong answer to this question can be supported with quotes and well-known anecdotes. A weak answer is so general it could apply to the figurehead of any company. I like this question because it tests knowledge of the corporate culture in a way that stretches beyond the company's reputation. Just going through the exercise can provide a deeper, more personal appreciation of the companies that interest you.

I was in the midst of my second round of interviews at Leo Burnett when I was asked this question. What has always struck me about the agency is the ongoing, powerful presence of its founder. Although Leo died in the early 1970s, you can almost hear the question, "What would Leo think?" echo in the corridors, cubicles, and conference rooms. Even in death, Leo remains the guardian of the agency's ideas. He maintains a quiet watch as his devotees "reach for the stars." After thinking about this for a few moments, the person who seemed most similar in character was Obi-Wan (Old Ben) Kenobi—Luke Skywalker's mentor in the Star Wars trilogy.

Like Leo, Obi-Wan had a quiet influence until he intentionally lost a battle with Darth Vader and the Dark Side. His last words to Vader were:

> "If you strike me down, I shall become more powerful than you can possibly imagine."

Naturally, Vader killed him anyway. True to his word, Obi-Wan became the powerful spiritual leader of Luke Skywalker and the remaining Jedi Knights.

Like Obi-Wan, Leo's presence engages in constant battle with the Dark Side. Before he retired, Leo warned that he too might be forced to return from beyond to do battle with the forces of evil—mediocrity, complacency, and greed. Leo insisted that the company stay true to its mission as long as his name appeared on the door. Otherwise, he threatened to "materialize" and "rub it out" himself (from the speech *"When to Take My Name off the Door"*). Fortunately, that hasn't been necessary.

The Adjective Questions

About 20 minutes into the interview, I ask the "adjective questions." These are often the most important questions of the interview because of the insights they can provide.

"What are five adjectives your best friend might use to describe you?"

In this case, my objective is straightforward. I want to know how aware this person is of the impressions they make on others. Most people do well on the "best friend" question because they know why people like them. Occasionally, someone will throw in a few adjectives like "detail-oriented" and "punctual." When this happens, I respond:

> "This is your best friend we're talking about here. If I called the person right now, I doubt that 'detail-oriented' would be mentioned as one of your most attractive qualities."

Don't include irrelevant personal strengths. Answer the question that was asked.

"Someone who doesn't know you well doesn't like you. What are five adjectives he or she might use to describe you?"

This is the most important question of the series. No matter who you are, there will always be people who don't know you or particularly like you. Are you guilty of sending unintentionally negative signals? Be honest, but be sensible. "Mean-spirited" may be a way people describe you, but don't expect me to reward you for the insight.

Later in the interview, I'll use your adjectives in a work-related question:

"You've noticed that a new member of your team has become standoffish. It occurs to you that this person perceives you as:

- *arrogant*
- *driven*
- *withdrawn*
- *critical*
- *condescending*

How would you handle the situation?"

This question is meant to assess how objective, honest, and proactive you are. The ability to build good working relationships with people who may or may not like you is critical in business. Interpersonal skills can be your greatest strength or your biggest obstacle. Make them a strength.

"What are five adjectives I might use to describe you?"

As someone who doesn't know you well, I want to know how you think I perceive you. Overly self-conscious candidates rarely have a clue what I think. They are too busy worrying about how uncomfortable they are. It's normal to be nervous. Just stay alert to the impressions you create.

"You've known me now for about 25 minutes. What are five adjectives you might use to describe me?"

Your response to this question provides a glimpse at your ability to interact with unfamiliar people. This is important because, in almost any executive position, you will be asked to present yourself, your ideas, or your products and services to unfamiliar audiences. When this happens, it is important to make fast and relatively accurate judgments about their needs, interests, and perceptions.

Beyond the adjectives

Finding appropriate adjectives for any of the questions is only part of the answer. I often probe deeper into the origin of particular traits. For example, when I ask for five adjectives your best friend would use to describe you, I may ask you to elaborate.

Suppose your best friend would describe you as "colorful, fun, trustworthy, driven, and happy." Fun, trustworthy, and happy are self-explanatory. Colorful and driven are not. What makes you this way? If you have already done the thinking, you won't struggle with adjectives or examples to support your statements. Otherwise, you'll waste valuable interview time reflecting on aspects of your personality that should already be familiar to you.

"Do you have any questions for me?"

This is the time to remind yourself that you have a responsibility to interview the company. It is imperative that you ask meaningful questions. To help you understand why this is so important, an actual case study entitled "Choosing Your Boss" is included at the end of this section.

Questions to ask them:

Whatever you do, don't ask people how they spend a typical day. It's both expected and trite. Instead, consider the following:

"What do you wish all applicants knew about this company?"

This is one of the best ways to uncover valuable information because it does not beg for a positive or negative response. It is entirely up to the interviewer's interpretation. If several people at a company respond negatively, morale may be low. On the other hand, you may hear what a wonderful, supportive, family-oriented environment it is. Whatever the case, you'll be able to make a more informed decision when you get an offer.

"If you could change anything about this company, what would it be and how would you go about changing it?"

This is a good question to ask everyone because it may reveal underlying dissatisfaction. Are employees empowered or powerless? If everyone has complaints and no one believes that change is possible, expect to feel the same frustration if you accept the job. Ideally, you will find a healthy environment in which employees are empowered to identify problems and champion solutions.

"Are raises and promotions, in your opinion, based on tenure or performance?"

What you want is the interviewer's opinion rather than the company line. Raises should be based on performance. But, as many companies vigilantly control costs, you might find that tenure is a more important factor. Given the human tendency to use salary as a measure of success, it's important to know what you can realistically expect.

Imagine the following scenario. After one year on the job, you receive an outstanding evaluation and a small pay raise. How do you feel about the possibility that you may not be eligible for another raise for eighteen months? Imagine further that your current boss is a particularly difficult evaluator and you didn't receive high enough marks to warrant a raise. Can you wait another year or two before you get a raise? How would you stay motivated?

The final assessment

More often than not, ill-prepared candidates make my job easier by eliminating themselves. On the other hand, if my overall impression is favorable, it becomes a matter of using the interview, résumé, cover letter, and writing sample to assess enthusiasm, talent, and potential.

As you might have guessed, the process is subjective, not scientific. The deciding factor—even with great candidates—may be as intangible as a gut feeling. However, close calls are rare. More often than not, candidates miss the cut because of inadequate preparation and other factors well within their control.

CASE STUDY

The Importance of Choosing Your Boss

All job hunters—regardless of age, education, or experience—are solely responsible for their own happiness. Some people are so desperate to find a job, and so anxious to please potential employers that they don't ask hard questions. However, these same questions can earn the respect of people who prefer employees with a backbone.

"Laura" had been out of school less than two years when she considered her first career change. At first, Laura was confused by her own sense of urgency. After some reflection, Laura discovered that the feeling wasn't caused by a profound dislike for her job. Like many young people, she just didn't feel she was where she needed to be. She wanted to "get on with it." Gradually, she realized that her current job put her in an enviable position. She had the luxury of waiting for the right opportunity.

The dilemma

In the course of her search, Laura was invited to meet with an executive who was expanding his department. Before her appointment, she conducted a series of informational interviews to learn more about the company. Although the job seemed interesting, she was surprised to hear people describe a widespread morale problem. What disturbed her even more was the fact that people in different departments all blamed the same person—the executive Laura was scheduled to meet.

At first, Laura rationalized her reluctance to discuss the issue during her initial meeting by saying: "I don't want to make waves. I know myself well enough to know that I can work with almost anybody. This isn't an issue." As the interview approached, she sensed a conflict between her mind and her body. Her rational mind continued to say, "Don't worry. This is a great opportunity." Her body, which felt tense and uncertain, delivered the opposite message.

Listening to her body

In an effort to understand her inner turmoil, Laura turned to meditation. She cleared her mind and began to listen to her body. After a few minutes, a picture formed in her mind. She could see herself standing on the edge of a cliff overlooking an abyss. Almost immediately, Laura associated the edge of the cliff with the hopelessness she felt before getting her first job offer. She could feel her body shift slightly, but somehow "hopelessness" didn't quite fit. Laura no longer saw herself as a potential victim of forces beyond her control. Instead, she felt both trapped and responsible. This led to a profound shift in her awareness and understanding. Specifically, Laura knew that if she was wrong about her ability to work effectively with this person, she would have no one to blame but herself. From this came two crucial insights:

- If the prospect of discussing employee morale seemed difficult now, it would only get harder when she became the person's subordinate.

CASE STUDY (continued)

- She could mention the issue as an observation—without assessing blame—and ask the executive what plans, if any, were in place to address it.

Difficult questions, educated choices

Despite Laura's best efforts at diplomacy, the executive became agitated at the mention of employee morale. When he denied that a problem even existed, Laura had to face the truth. The most interesting job in the world couldn't offset the unnecessary stress of having this person for a boss.

Shortly after the interview, Laura decided to withdraw from consideration. However, not wanting to miss an opportunity for growth, she called the executive to hear his impressions. He shared the following contradictory observations:

- She was "overly confident" for a person with "such limited experience."

- She wasn't the right person for the job. She was, he feared, someone who would "get bored too quickly."

The first statement, by itself, might be a valid observation. But it doesn't make sense given his second statement. A person at risk of becoming "bored too quickly" is more likely to be overqualified than underqualified.

A final challenge

At this point, Laura could have called the friend who arranged the interview, thanked him for his efforts, and focused on other opportunities. Somehow, that didn't seem like the right approach. He wasn't just a friend, he was the president of the company. Had their roles been reversed and he was the one who uncovered potential issues, she would definitely want to know—no matter how difficult it was to hear. Furthermore, this wasn't about her. The job wasn't right for her anyway.

To Laura's credit, she didn't dwell on the negative. Instead, she focused her conversation with the president on what would be possible given effective leadership and enthusiastic employee participation. She found comfort not only in his positive reaction, but also in the satisfaction of acting in accordance with her highest values.

Creating a space for opportunity

Without this discussion, the president would have known only that Laura wasn't interested in the position. As a result, he might not have considered her for future openings. By sharing her concerns, she left nothing to interpretation. As Laura prepared to leave, he tore a page from his notebook and gave her the name of another person to contact. A few weeks later, that person became her boss.

> MORE TROUBLE IS CAUSED IN THIS WORLD BY INDISCRETE ANSWERS THAN BY INDISCRETE QUESTIONS.
>
> —SYDNEY J. HARRIS

> LISTEN CAREFULLY TO THE VOICE IN YOUR MIND AS IT IS GETTING READY TO MAKE A COMMENT, AND THINK TO YOURSELF, "WHY AM I SAYING THIS?" . . . IS WHAT I AM ABOUT TO SAY AN IMPROVEMENT OVER MAINTAINING SILENCE?
>
> —SYLVIA BOORSTEIN, "IT'S EASIER THAN YOU THINK: THE BUDDHIST WAY TO HAPPINESS"

Other Interviewing Styles

Generally speaking, every interviewer should strive to answer the same questions:

- "Can this person excel at our company?"
- "Do I want this person on my team?"

While there are as many different approaches as there are interviewers, your preparation for each will be the same. You must know yourself. This includes an arsenal of concrete examples that demonstrate your strengths, commitment, and abilities.

Create your own "package of ideas"

As an applicant, your top priority is to manage the impression you create. Regardless of the interviewer's style, you need to communicate the same core skills to every interviewer. Once you have a "package of ideas" that represents the essence of your potential, bring it to every interview.

As an interview progresses, fill the package one idea at a time. Near the end of the interview, many recruiters ask: "Is there anything else I should know?" At that point, finish filling the package. If you have already covered the main ideas either summarize your qualifications or add a few secondary details. To say, "I think we have covered everything" is a mistake because the question is often asked to give you the opportunity to "close the deal."

Leaving a complete package of ideas can be difficult in some interview situations. If you're running out of time, take charge:

> "I noticed that we are almost out of time. Since your job here today is to assess my potential as an employee of this company, I would like to mention a few specifics that are relevant to your evaluation. Does that work for you?"

I can't imagine an interviewer who would not be impressed with such a direct and honest approach. Once you get agreement, fill in whatever gaps remain and conclude by asking a few direct questions.

If you find it uncomfortable to use this approach, it might help to remember that you are doing both yourself and the interviewer a favor. The fact that you are in this predicament is, in all probability, a result of the interviewer's lack of skill and experience. You may even take some of the pressure off when you refocus the conversation.

The stress interview

For whatever reason, some interviewers do nothing to make candidates feel comfortable. Instead, they do everything imaginable to make them squirm. Although it's less common, it is a style you should be prepared to handle.

Stress interviews take many forms. Some interviewers ask rapid-fire questions. Others challenge every answer. Whatever the tactic, it's nothing more than a game. Approach it that way. Think of it as an ongoing battle between you and an opponent whose sole objective is to search for inconsistencies in your answers. Don't let them put words in your mouth. If you hesitate or change your mind, you've lost.

Before you spend any time worrying about stress interviews, read the next section carefully. It could change the way you think about stress.

The ultimate (and fair) test of preparation

Most interviews are structured around a series of questions that each recruiter uses to assess candidates. However, some insightful recruiters use untraditional methods to achieve the same objectives. Because you can't be prepared for every eventuality, your only choice is to be prepared for any eventuality.

One executive I know doesn't ask any questions at all. Instead, he gives a brief introduction and allows the candidate to run the meeting. This typically includes an impromptu presentation by the candidate as well as questions for the recruiter. Not coincidentally, this is the same challenge that executives in his firm face every day. Is this approach demanding? Absolutely. Is it unfair? Definitely not. Is it stressful? That depends on the person.

Stress, if it exists, is a function of the candidate's expectations and interpretations. To see how this works, imagine how different people might respond to the interviewer described above.

Candidate 1:
Expectation: The interviewer will ask questions, evaluate my answers, and make a hiring decision.

Response/Interpretation: "Wow! I can't believe he isn't going to ask me any questions. He's really putting my on the spot. This is pressure."

Candidate 2:
Expectation: The interviewer's primary objective is to evaluate my potential given the needs of the company. His method will be a matter of personal preference.

Response/Interpretation: "What a great opportunity! I've done my homework. I know what qualities are important to this company. And I know how I have demonstrated potential in those areas. This will be easier than I thought."

In each case, the executive's behavior was the same. Only the expectations and interpretations differed. This example is important because it reveals that stress is an internal phenomenon rather than an external one.

It is interesting to note that this entire discussion was generated by an approach to interviewing that can be summed up in two words—sell yourself.

Questions, questions, and more questions

Below is a list of common interview questions. Some have a single, relatively obvious objective. Others are used to assess multiple attributes (e.g., time management, prioritizing, managing expectations). All are questions that you might encounter.

MORE INTERVIEW QUESTIONS AND TOPICS

- Tell me about yourself.
- Why are you here?
- You are asked to write a one-page ad for yourself. What is the headline?
- What are your greatest strengths?
- What are your weaknesses?
- What one thing would you _not_ want me to know about you?
- A client has given you 10 projects, but you only have time to do three well. What do you do?
- What color is your brain?
- Sell me this paperclip.
- What is one of your greatest accomplishments?
- Continuum questions (i.e., Rate yourself on a continuum between the following adjectives or phrases.)

"Tell me about yourself"

This may be the vaguest and most difficult of all interview questions. If you had a particularly interesting childhood that impacted the person you are today, you might begin there. In any case, make it clear where you are going. Otherwise, the interviewer will be forced to interrupt your life story when it's clear that you aren't using the question to your advantage.

"Why are you here?"

The confrontational nature of this question begs a direct and concise response. In effect, the interviewer is saying:

> "I value my time. Let's get right to the point. Convince me that we should be having this conversation."

If you already know that you want the company to make you an offer, simply explain how your skills match their needs. On the other hand, if your mission is to learn more about the company, you might say:

> "Overall, there seems to be a good match between my skills and your needs. My goal today is to determine if this is truly a good fit."

The last time anyone asked me this question, it caught me by surprise because the circumstances were so unusual. I had been working for several months on a freelance marketing project so I wasn't exactly in interview mode when I met the new senior vice president of marketing. Without smiling, he looked me in the eye and in an abrupt, but professional way asked, "Why are you here?" After a deep breath, I outlined my experiences and objectives as they related to the needs of the company. Highlighting the company's needs rather than my strengths also helped to take some of the pressure off. But I'd be lying if I didn't admit that it took time to regain my composure.

"You are asked to write a one-page ad for yourself. What is the headline?"

The interviewer wants to know how well you know the product (you) and its benefits (the reasons you would be great at this company). Combine the product and benefit in a short, impactful headline. It doesn't have to be clever, but it should demonstrate that you understand the concept of positioning.

Although this question is particularly appropriate for advertising, it could be used in almost any interview. Whatever the position, you headline should demonstrate an understanding of the needs of the company.

"What are your greatest strengths?"

This is another opportunity to fill your "package of ideas." Use key words and phrases that correspond to the needs of the company (e.g., resourcefulness, problem-solving ability, strategic thinking). Any time you can sell yourself unabashedly, do it. Be confident, concise, and support your statements with personal examples.

"What are your weaknesses?"

Few questions generate as much pre- and post-interview conversation as this. While the concept (i.e., self-awareness) is valid, the question is so predictable it's become meaningless.

A mediocre interviewer will ask this question simply because it is a "classic" interview question. A more seasoned interviewer will ask it because he or she hasn't found a better way to assess how well you know yourself. As discussed previously, the following question comes closer to revealing the truth.

> "Someone who doesn't know you well doesn't like you. What are five adjectives he or she might use to describe you?"

Fortunately, you don't have to know why the question was asked to handle it effectively. Rather than disclosing weaknesses that could damn you to a life of unemployment, answer the following questions:

> "Given the qualities that are critical for success, in what area would you most like to improve? What are you doing to make that happen?"

Provide evidence that you have worked on the areas you identified. If you haven't already done so, make a commitment to improve yourself both personally and professionally. Otherwise, your first on-the-job evaluation is not going to be an adventure you will be anxious to repeat.

"What one thing would you not want me to know about you?"

This is a ridiculous variation of the ever-popular question: "What is your biggest weakness?" Handle it as you would the "weakness" question.

"A client has given you 10 projects, but you only have time to do three well. What do you do?"

Although I have made every effort to provide strategies rather than specific answers, I will make an exception in this case. In a sense, this isn't a fair question because it puts a person with no work experience in a hypothetical situation unlike any he or she has ever faced.

In this case, the most common pitfall is an incorrect assumption. What entry-level candidates don't necessarily know is that professional life allows a much greater freedom to juggle priorities than they experienced as students. In school, the ability to negotiate extended deadlines is almost nonexistent. In the business world, flexibility is available to those who negotiate.

To operate under the assumption that all 10 deadlines are firm sends a powerful negative message. In effect, this indicates a willingness to sacrifice quality for expediency. This is a trade-off that can create confusion, resentment, and disappointment. For this reason, this is as much a question about leadership as it is about prioritizing and time management.

One of the best approaches to a dilemma like this is to seek the advice of your boss. If the boss is the source of the problem, this conversation is even more important because expressing concerns openly is an important part of teamwork, leadership, and communication.

As you consider the alternatives, keep in mind that work, at most corporations, is a team sport. Every decision necessarily impacts the whole team. For this reason, effective leaders make sure that everyone understands the dilemma and has an opportunity to offer input. Ideas and solutions can come from anywhere, but they will only emerge when the team feels empowered. Having said that, the interviewer might probe further:

> "Let's imagine that you brought the team and client together only to hear the client say that all 10 projects share equal priority and must be completed by the same date. What now?"

In a situation like this, the demanding client must assume some responsibility—provided, of course, that your company didn't cause the problem in the first place. At this point, you should weigh the relative merits of each project and make a recommendation that outlines expected results by project. If the client doesn't agree with the recommendation, they must either state an alternative or communicate specific objections your team can address. One way or another, everyone must understand and accept the action plan. Uncertainty is not acceptable.

If negotiations fail to yield an acceptable solution, stand firm and promise only what you can realistically achieve. You may have to dig into a reserve supply of courage, honesty, and Zantac—but you'll be glad you did. The value of maintaining your professional integrity and the morale of your co-workers is far greater than the risk of upsetting a client. Unreasonable clients are the toddlers of the professional world. If you make sacrifices to satisfy them this week, how can you possibly tell them "no" next week?

"What color is your brain?"

This is strictly a fun question that begs for a creative answer. The answer itself doesn't matter. What matters is your confidence. Just be ready to defend your answer. If you say, "I like to think of my brain as a rainbow of bright colors that blend to match my experiences," have specific colors and experiences in mind. It's better to be enthusiastic and bizarre than self-conscious and uncertain.

"Sell me this paper clip."

This is a legitimate question for any career because every business has customers and competitors. To survive, it must also have meaningful competitive benefits. What are they?

Whenever you are asked to "sell" or "market" a particular product in an interview, approach the problem as if you are the first person ever to see the object. Be enthusiastic about the different uses you discover:

Paper clip uses/benefits

- Use: It can hold papers together.
  Benefit: You'll save time being more organized and efficient.

- Use: It can function as a weight on a paper airplane.
  Benefit: By adding weight, the plane will fly farther and you'll have more fun.

Once you have identified the uses and benefits, you will be in a better position to describe potential customers, competitors, and the qualities that make paper clips superior (i.e., the product positioning).

"What is one of your greatest accomplishments?"

A good interviewer will probe accomplishments the same way he or she assesses problem-solving ability. Structure your answer by describing:

- the obstacle/challenge

- possible courses of action

- specific tactics

- quantifiable results

If you skip a step, expect to be grilled on it. For example, if the accomplishment you describe relates to superior customer service, the interviewer might ask the following questions:

- "What specific traits do customers value most in you?"

- "I would imagine that your customers have different levels of satisfaction. What would one of your least satisfied customers say?"

Continuum questions

This approach asks that you place yourself on an imaginary range between two specific traits or qualities. Despite its popularity, this line of questioning is artificial, contrived, and shallow. To truly appreciate the flaw in this approach, imagine yourself as the interviewer. You have just asked a candidate to place herself on a continuum between strategic and tactical. She responds:

"I definitely fall on the strategic end of the continuum."

Is this the right answer? If "strategic" is what you wanted to hear, her answer was probably correct. But what did you really learn? Even if she pinpoints an exact location on the continuum, so what? You still haven't learned anything. Self-appraisal without example is meaningless. She has simply described herself using one of two adjectives you provided. Now, aren't you glad you asked?

Structuring your response

Adjectives on a continuum typically fall into three categories:

- positive/positive

- neutral/positive

- negative/negative

In some cases, it won't be clear whether the words are positive, negative, or neutral. If you are unsure, think about the words as they relate to the specific needs of the company and make your best guess.

Positive/positive or neutral/positive: If the decision is between two positive adjectives, the middle ground might seem safest. It isn't. By asking the question, the interviewer wants you to take a stand. Use a four-step approach:

- Determine which attribute is more important.

- Acknowledge the importance of each relative to the job requirements.

- Place yourself to the left or right of center (toward the more important adjective).

- Give a personal example that demonstrates the more important attribute.

In some cases, even a theoretical continuum is of limited use. The strategic/tactical continuum is an excellent example of this. These approaches are interdependent rather than mutually exclusive. The ability to get work done is meaningless if your tactics are not based on a sound strategy. Likewise, what good are strategic skills if you lack the tactical ability to champion actionable solutions?

Negative/Negative: When faced with two negative adjectives and no continuum, you don't necessarily have to answer the question. For example, one interviewer didn't give me a continuum, he simply asked:

"Are you the kind of person who works to live or lives to work?"

Before responding, I asked for clarification:

"Are you allowing for a continuum between the two?"

Unsympathetically, he replied:

"No. Choose one."

Because I guessed that he was trying to assess my passion for advertising, I chose "live to work." In hindsight, picking either extreme was a mistake. I should have said:

"Given that we aren't allowing for a continuum, I honestly don't feel comfortable picking either of two dysfunctional extremes."

This was the truth. I just didn't have the guts to say it at the time.

Handling Inappropriate Questions

Questions about religion, ethnicity, marital status, or family planning are illegal in any recruiting circumstance. The fact that many interviews are not conducted by professional recruiters is never an excuse for illegal, inappropriate, or sexist comments or questions. Unfortunately, because these questions do arise from time to time, you'll need to be ready. How you respond may depend on two factors:

- **Whether or not the interviewer's approach is out of character for the company.**

    Is this an isolated event or have you noticed other examples of poor judgment and unprofessional conduct?

- **How badly you want the job.**

    Are you willing to remove yourself from consideration solely on principle? Is it possible to diplomatically avoid the question with your integrity intact?

Three tactics

In handling inappropriate questions, there are three tactics you might consider. Whichever you choose, be professional and move on quickly.

1. Gently remind the interviewer that the question is both inappropriate and irrelevant.

You may be absolutely correct and a pillar of diplomacy, but that won't change the fact that you may involuntarily remove yourself from consideration. Of course, that may be for the best.

2. Rephrase the question in a non-offensive way before responding.

Perhaps you are a woman who has just been asked, "Do you think you will want children in the next three to five years?" Using this approach, you might respond:

> "It sounds as if you have concerns about my commitment to my career. I am extremely committed—I assure you. Whether or not I decide to have children will in no way impact my dedication or performance."

IN SKATING OVER THIN ICE, OUR SAFETY IS IN OUR SPEED.

—EMERSON

FACTS DO NOT CEASE TO EXIST BECAUSE THEY ARE IGNORED.

—ALDOUS HUXLEY

Opposite:
Words & picture: Harry Wilson © 1996. From his forthcoming book of images and observations "I Wouldn't Have Missed It for Anything" (working title). Printed with permission.

3. **If you recognize the question as inappropriate and you don't strongly object, answer the question.**

Next steps

After the interview—preferably the same day—inform the company's human resources department of any questionable encounters. These are the people responsible for educating interviewers and discouraging unprofessional behavior.

We owe a serious debt of gratitude to business.

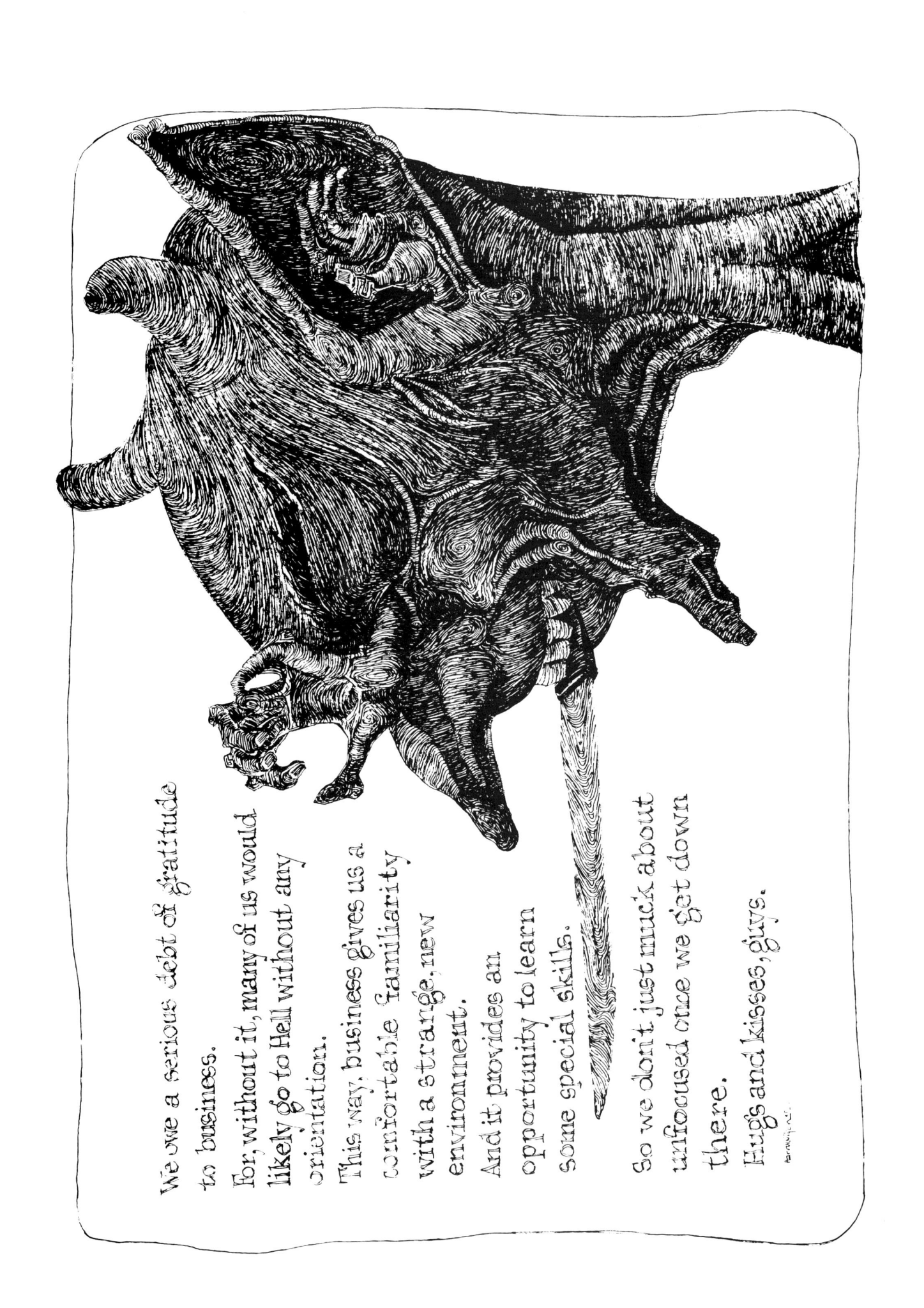

For, without it, many of us would likely go to Hell without any orientation.

This way, business gives us a comfortable familiarity with a strange, new environment.

And it provides an opportunity to learn some special skills.

So we don't just muck about unfocused once we get down there.

Hugs and kisses, guys.

CHAPTER 6

Improving Your Technique and Closing the Deal

Believe in Yourself

Job hunting can be an intense, highly competitive, ego-battering experience. What makes it even more stressful is the fact that energetic, motivated people, like yourself, often have traits that are both helpful and harmful. For example, high expectations can either contribute to your success or heighten your disappointment. To avoid this dilemma, commit yourself to a course of action rather than a specific outcome. For example, make the goal of your job search personal growth rather than a particular job offer. This way, you can emerge a stronger, more confident person whether or not you get a particular job. Developing this attitude is as challenging as it is helpful because it requires two elusive traits:

- A sincere desire for self-improvement

- The ability to appreciate your value as a human being

A sincere desire for self-improvement

This is the litmus test for potential. No matter who you are, there will always be room for improvement. Even the world's greatest athletes have coaches.

Seek constructive criticism

With the possible exception of the terminally unhappy and dissatisfied, most people are not comfortable vocalizing criticism. Your biggest challenge may to create a space in which people can view their insight as helpful rather than critical. Genuine curiosity, openness, and sincerity will be invaluable in this regard.

MOST PEOPLE ARE ABOUT AS HAPPY AS THEY MAKE UP THEIR MINDS TO BE.

—UNKNOWN

ADVERSITY INTRODUCES A MAN TO HIMSELF.

—UNKNOWN

As you listen to constructive criticism, be courteous and grateful. If the feedback surprises you, explore its origin. To avoid appearing confrontational or defensive, imagine yourself as an objective third party searching for the truth. For example, you might respond:

> "That's interesting. Perhaps you could share some of the specifics that led to that impression."

In some cases, the person's own experience may impact their interpretation more than your actual behavior. Or perhaps the impressions were consistent with your actions, but inconsistent with your intentions. This is the time to find out.

You might probe further by asking friends, family, and acquaintances what they see as your strengths and weaknesses. Just because you don't ask, doesn't mean they haven't thought about it.

Develop your talents

The desire to improve yourself does not always relate to a weakness in your character or ability. It can also reveal itself in your commitment to projects, hobbies, and other extracurricular activities.

One interviewer shocked me when he said that my commitment to piano lessons demonstrated my potential more strongly than any other experence. He was genuinely impressed that I had spent more than one year learning to play the first movement of Beethoven's *Grande Sonata Pathétique*. He loved the fact that I had that kind of dedication as a senior in high school. Actually, I don't think dedication is rare. Hobbies and interests inspire far greater passion. People just don't think to sell themselves on it.

Appreciating your value

Whatever happens, it is important to remember that your value as a person is absolutely separate from your ability to compete. It is only natural to want to be the best. Just be comfortable with the fact that there will always be people of greater and lesser ability. The only person to outperform is yourself.

A single important rejection or series of disappointments can humble even the most confident and secure person. It's always disheartening to know that you haven't met someone else's expectations. Nevertheless, take rejection for what it is—a fact of life. For people who never appreciate their self-worth, rejection is a license to quit. For others, it is an opportunity to reassess strengths, weaknesses, and goals.

When history repeats itself

Not long ago, I spoke with a person who had just been rejected by ten graduate programs for the second year in a row. To my surprise, he never thought to get feedback after his first rejections. Instead, he spent countless hours and hundreds of dollars repeating the same mistakes.

Like many people, he never imagined that a recruiter would take the time to discuss an individual application. The fact is, any organization that charges an application fee owes you at least that much. Otherwise, what assurance would you have that they didn't cash the check and throw the paperwork away? An application fee that doesn't buy a little constructive criticism should be refunded. Don't be shy.

EVERYONE IS PERFECTLY WILLING TO LEARN FROM UNPLEASANT EXPERIENCE—IF ONLY THE DAMAGE OF THE FIRST LESSON COULD BE REPAIRED.

—*LICHTENBERG*

Learning from Interviews

To leave an interview thinking, "Great, I nailed it!" or "I can't believe I blew it!" is a waste of time. Unless the interviewer shares his or her impressions, you will probably never know. Never use the interviewer's disposition as a gauge of your performance. Instead, ask yourself the following questions:

- What did the interviewer ask?

- How concisely and completely did I answer each question?

- What, if anything, caught me by surprise?

- How can I better prepare for future interviews?

- What did I learn?

Twenty-two and never been interviewed

My first interview took place on campus during my senior year in college. Although I have repressed the event itself, a productive post-interview evaluation would focus only on the short list of things I did right. Most of my mistakes could be attributed to a lack of experience, preparation, and confidence.

My most serious mistake was strategic. I should never have scheduled my first interview with Leo Burnett—the company I wanted most. At the very least, I should have done a mock interview with the career counselors. Somehow, this never occurred to me.

When I finally realized my mistake, I was face-to-face with the recruiter. My confidence was nowhere to be found. Having done a relatively thorough self-analysis, I knew some of the strengths to emphasize, but I was far from convincing. Worse, I couldn't stop shaking long enough to smile.

My performance was a surprise to everyone—including me. The career counselors didn't dream I would need help interviewing because they knew me as an outgoing, focused, and confident person. My abominable performance was saved only by the recruiter's open-mindedness. I will be forever grateful to that wonderful man for seeing beyond my trembling exterior.

Several weeks after the interview, Leo Burnett flew me to Chicago for a full day of interviews. Not surprisingly, the recruiter encouraged me to relax. Somehow he must have known I would never survive seven hours of shaking and sweating.

The full-round interviews

For some reason, I didn't find it necessary to sell myself in each and every interview. As a result, Burnett didn't find it necessary to hire me. I told the recruiter (in a nice way) that the company was making a terrible mistake. He replied, "That may be true. Do something else for a year and try again. We never shut the door on anyone."

When I reapplied after graduate school, another recruiter shared some of the written evaluations from my first full-round. To my surprise, the individual decisions were exactly opposite of what I would have predicted.

The interview I thought went the worst was with the only person who recommended hiring me. I had written the interview off because I was convinced that the person didn't like me. I'll never forget how uncomfortable I felt when she challenged my answer to the question: "Why advertising?" With a look of frustration, she said:

"That sounds like a rehearsed answer—like someone told you to say that."

Shocked, I replied:

"I'm sorry you feel that way. It is the truth."

Now I realize that my original answer may or may not have sounded rehearsed. It may just have been her way of testing my confidence. Either way, the lesson is the same. Be positive and direct. Tell the truth. Defend your answers. And don't try to guess what the interviewer thinks about you.

The second full-round

During the second full-round at Burnett, I sold myself in every interview. Several people even asked:

"Why do you think we didn't hire you last year?"

Fortunately, I had done more than a little thinking about it. As it happened, I had spent too much time trying to make sure everybody liked me and not enough time convincing people that I could add value to the company. Having made the first cut, I mistakenly assumed that interviewers would automatically know I had the skills to succeed. That, however, is not the way it works. I should have approached every interview as if it were my only opportunity at the agency. In hindsight, the people who interviewed and rejected me reached the only reasonable conclusion. Had I been the interviewer, I wouldn't have hired me either.

Suboptimal interviews

If you are absolutely convinced that the interviewer's opinion has turned against you—and it's more than just a challenge of your resolve—approach the issue politely:

> "Before we go any further, am I correct in thinking that you have some concerns I should address?"

For this to work, your delivery must be confident, sincere, and direct. If you sound unsure of yourself, it could raise questions about your leadership and communication skills. If your assessment is accurate, the interviewer will probably be impressed by your direct approach and perceptiveness. You might even sell yourself back into consideration.

When to cancel or cut an interview short

In the event of an illness, family emergency, or any other circumstance serious enough to hinder your performance, call the company immediately and reschedule. For situations that arise after the interview has begun, you'll need a different approach.

Although I don't recommend it as a key strategy in your arsenal, there may be times when your best move is to interrupt the interview, cut your losses, and attempt to reschedule. Since you might be having trouble imagining a scenario, I'll share a personal example.

The meltdown

As I made my way toward the campus center at Northwestern University for an early morning interview, my head was filled with the usual fantasies: immediate positive feedback, job offers, professional success, and infinite happiness. I don't remember feeling ill, but apparently I was.

After a short wait, the recruiter introduced herself, smiled brightly, and led me to an oversized conference room. The floor-to-ceiling bay windows on the far side of the room revealed a spectacular Lake Michigan sunrise. As I sat down, the huge windows magnified the already intense rays beating down on my face. I winced and began to sweat. And sweat. And sweat. I felt worse with each moment, but I kept going.

Fifteen or twenty torturous minutes into the interview, I stood up and struggled to remove my jacket. At that point, I should have explained that I felt ill, apologized for the inconvenience, and asked to reschedule. Instead, I ignored a rather obvious problem.

By the time I peeled off my jacket, I was so delirious I couldn't remember what question I was answering. Meanwhile, sweat poured down my face and formed a puddle on the floor around me. After forty-five minutes, my hair and clothes were soaked. Nothing was even dry enough to wipe the sweat away so I could shake hands and say good-bye. Frosty the Snowman melted faster, but not by much.

As I slid outside, I saw a horrified expression on the next candidate. My appearance left him speechless and traumatized. Realizing what must have been going through his mind, I laughed and said, "Don't worry, she's really nice."

Because I wasn't honest about feeling ill, I performed poorly and eliminated myself from consideration. The recruiter may not have allowed me to reschedule, but I would have been no worse for asking.

> *THERE CAN BE NO REAL FREEDOM WITHOUT THE FREEDOM TO FAIL.*
>
> —ERIC HOFFER

> *THE GREATEST MISTAKE YOU CAN MAKE IN LIFE IS TO BE CONTINUALLY FEARING THAT YOU WILL MAKE ONE.*
>
> —ELBERT HUBBARD

Beyond Nervousness

For many, interviews never seem to get easier. Even the word itself can inspire fear. While it's good to be slightly nervous before an interview, you don't want to be so nervous that you can't relax. Just remember, it's your relaxed and enthusiastic self employers are looking to hire. Show them that person.

Solid preparation may be the best natural cure for nervousness. If you have done a comprehensive self-analysis and matched your skills to the company's needs, there is no question you can't handle.

When your mind goes blank

If you have taken a moment to think about a question and you still don't have an answer, be honest:

"For some reason I am struggling to come up with an answer. Would you mind rephrasing the question?"

Honesty is important because it:

- can loosen the vice grip of embarrassment and uncertainty.
- buys time to think about the question.
- communicates sincerity.

Overcoming insecurity

If insufficient preparation is not a factor in your nervousness, you might be facing a more general insecurity. If so, that is what you need to confront.

The insecurity I felt in interviews extended to public speaking, group meetings, and other events in which I felt vulnerable to criticism. I didn't realize that the expectations I wasn't living up to were my own. This became clear when a concerned friend asked:

"What, exactly, do you tell yourself before an interview?"

Gradually, I began to face the insecurity. Looking inward, I understood its origin.

All of my life, I have done well in almost every pursuit—at least the ones I considered important. Even grad school wasn't especially difficult. Unfortunately, by generalizing these experiences, I taught myself to expect that desire alone would lead to success. What I created was the perfect recipe for disappointment.

By punishing myself unnecessarily, I turned every interview and presentation into moments of sheer terror. The fear—and my ability to control it—seemed wholly unpredictable. Without warning, I would either shake visibly or ramble energetically. Either way, I was difficult to follow. As a result, my every presentation looked like a panic attack.

I basically had two alternatives. I could forge my way through life dreading every presentation or expose my insecurities to the world and drive them out of my life. Choosing the latter proved to be a wonderful and liberating experience.

From Dale Carnegie to Players' Workshop

Enrolling in the Dale Carnegie course in human relations and public speaking gave me the courage to accept another, more difficult challenge—improv classes at Second City's Players Workshop. For one year, our class met every Saturday for three hours. For some, this was one step on the long road to Second City, Saturday Night Live, or stand-up comedy. For others, it was just a fun way to spend a Saturday afternoon.

The art of improvisation

What attracted me to improvisation was the promise that I could be trained to be more objective and less self-conscious. Nevertheless, I was terrified because I had almost no experience. Except for a few class shows in grade school, I'd never been on stage.

What I love about improv is that it replaces terror with excitement. It also opens the mind, increases spontaneity, and demonstrates the value of teamwork. Better still, Leo Burnett paid for most of it. (The agency considers improv to be so valuable that it is the only noncredit class that qualifies for reimbursement.)

The "big eye"

During the first few classes, I struggled with what our coach called the "big eye." This is the voice in your head that, in moments of extreme self-consciousness, shouts:

"Don't do that, you'll look like an idiot. People will make fun of you!"

After a few weeks, this voice quiets to a whisper. Meanwhile, your adventurous, childlike self learns to take chances, make mistakes, and have fun. This creates the space to be yourself in uncomfortable and unfamiliar situations. As such, it is particularly important for interviews because it can help people recognize confrontational questions as a game rather than a personal attack.

Why improv works

The objective of improv is to create a scene (i.e., location, characters, and relationships) without the benefit of planning or props. If the players need a particular object, they simply "discover" it. At the start of a scene, three or four students will be on stage when the instructor will asks the rest of the class:

"Who are they? Where are they? And what are they doing?"

From different corners of the room, voices might chime:

"They're penguins."
"At the zoo."
"And it's feeding time!"

Within seconds, the situation is established. The instructor says, "Go" and the scene begins.

As seamlessly as possible, the players establish the relationships and initiate activities based on the suggestions from the audience. By watching, listening, and involving themselves fully, the players' attention naturally slips into the scene they are creating. To focus on the actions of the team and still be consumed by self-consciousness is literally impossible.

The same is true for interviewing. Involve yourself fully in the conversation. Watch for nonverbal signals. You won't have any energy left to be nervous. You may even enjoy yourself.

Salary Negotiation

At the entry-level, your opportunity to negotiate is limited. Nevertheless, you should be prepared to handle the topic confidently—if and when it arises. Compensation is too important an issue to treat lightly. In general terms, think of salary negotiation as a poker game you play with your future income. To win, you must know what to say and when to say it. Above all, don't show your cards to anyone.

Handling salary questions

Before responding to a salary inquiry, ask yourself two questions:

- What stage of the interview process is this?

- Is the person asking the question a key decision maker?

What stage of the interview process is this?

If an offer hasn't been extended, don't discuss salary. A convincing response that avoids a premature discussion is this:

> "At this point, I am more interested in whether or not this is a good mutual fit. Let's make sure we have addressed all issues of compatibility before we get to the specifics of salary."

Is the person asking the question a key decision maker?

More than once, I have heard from candidates who were grilled on salary questions by low-level employees who have little say in hiring decisions and no input in salary negotiations. They probably just get a weird thrill pretending they have authority. Your challenge is to shift the focus to more salient issues. For example, counter with another question:

> "You do pay a fair and competitive salary, don't you?"

This response is effective whether or not the person is a decision maker because it puts the pressure on the interviewer—where it belongs. If the interviewer pursues the issue, you have two options. First, if you have outstanding questions (other than salary) that will impact your decision to accept or reject an offer, address them immediately:

THE BIGGEST HUMAN TEMPTATION IS... TO SETTLE FOR TOO LITTLE.

—*THOMAS MERTON*

ONLY WHEN THE LAST TREE HAS DIED, THE LAST RIVER POISONED, AND THE LAST FISH BEEN CAUGHT, WILL WE REALIZE THAT WE CANNOT EAT MONEY.

—*19TH CENTURY CREE INDIAN SAYING*

"Before we discuss salary, I'd like to take the next several minutes to ask a few more questions about the company and the position."

If you have no further questions, and you know the person is a decision-maker, take a deep breath and begin. Otherwise, arrange a meeting with the appropriate person.

The psychology of negotiation

For many people, salary is an emotionally-charged issue inextricably tied to their self-image. This is unfortunate because there is no correlation between income, happiness, and your value as a human being. The inability to separate self from salary is also one of the greatest obstacles to effective negotiation.

To replace emotion with objectivity, I often pretend that I'm representing someone other than myself. This way, I become less attached to a specific outcome and view it as the fun game that it is. This confident, almost distant approach has two primary benefits:

- It prevents me from making unnecessary concessions.

- It encourages the other party to work harder toward a deal.

The challenge is to be a tough negotiator without being an obstructionist. On the other extreme, don't confuse desperation with enthusiasm. You are a risk to yourself if your attitude communicates any of the following messages:

- "I'd work here for any salary."

- "I can't live without this job."

- "My life and my happiness are at stake."

If you even get the job—which would be doubtful at this point—this perception will earn you the worst deal imaginable. If you jump at any offer, the company will know you would have accepted less. This can have a substantial negative impact on your perceived value to the company.

The two most forgotten rules of negotiation

Some people are so excited by offers, and so intimidated by interviews, that they abandon common sense when they should be negotiating. "Yes," "Of course," and "That's fine" are not the first words uttered by skilled negotiators. When you begin negotiating, keep two rules in mind:

- Don't answer questions (or supply information) about your salary history.

- Don't quote specific figures.

Salary history

Believe it or not, your previous salary is irrelevant. Only two factors should be considered:

- your market value

- your value to the company

When asked about previous salary, diplomatically say:

> "I understand your curiosity. I also know that my prior compensation has no relevance to my value to this company. Nor will it impact my ability to excel in the position. If we clarify your expectations and my ability to meet them, I am confident that we can arrive at a fair salary."

The fact is, any company that is actively recruiting should have budgeted for the position. Furthermore, the company's ability or obligation to pay your salary has no connection to compensation agreements between you and a previous employer.

If you are still uncomfortable with the issue, imagine this: A house is for sale at an unspecified price. You like the house but you aren't confident that you can put an accurate value on it. Sensing your interest, the owner asks, "How much will the bank loan you?"

If you are smart, you won't respond. Your credit line at the bank has nothing to do with the value of the house. Answering the question makes no sense whatsoever because it gives the seller valuable information while the buyer receives nothing in return. From this point on, negotiation will favor the seller who now knows the buyer's upper limit. Meanwhile the seller's lowest acceptable price remains a mystery. The buyer hasn't even determined a possible price range. So it goes with salary negotiation.

Quoting specific figures

At the beginning of the negotiation, the company may be reluctant to quote a specific salary. If so, ask about the range. If you know the range, you will have a better chance of negotiating a salary on the higher end.

To quote a specific salary without any information about what the company might pay is a huge risk. If the company has budgeted $28,000 to $35,000 and you state a salary requirement above $35,000 or below $28,000, you can only lose. If the company knows they can hire you for $25,000, that's probably what they will pay. It won't matter that the range was higher. No one is in business to give money away.

If you state a salary requirement higher than the range, you could still lose. If the company's offer is competitive and you quote a salary outside the range, it will be obvious that you didn't do your homework. On the other hand, if you know you are worth the premium, defend your position.

Acceptable offers

An acceptable offer may come in one of two forms:

- within the expected range

- higher than the expected range

Offers within the expected range

When the company makes an offer in line with your expectations, keep your best poker face and say:

"Let me think about that for a minute."

Silence is an extremely powerful negotiating tool. You might spend the time planning ways to spend the cash. No one has to know. As far as the company knows, you are diligently working out a rough budget for yourself. After a minute or so, one of two things will happen:

- The person on the other side of the desk, growing uncomfortable in the silence, breaks and says: *"Of course, we could probably go as high as. . ."*

    If so, congratulations, you have just earned your first raise.

- The other person does nothing. In this case, smile and say:

    "That sounds reasonable. Let's discuss other specifics like vacation, insurance, profit-sharing, and bonuses."

Once you reach an acceptable offer, take at least one night before you commit. This is also a good way to avoid looking desperate.

Offers above the expected range

Silence can also have a wonderful impact on an already high salary because there may still be room to the upside. Therefore, the same rules apply. However, a salary that is significantly higher than industry standard may be a warning flag. One or more of the following could be true:

- The responsibilities of the job differ significantly from your expectations.

- The company has a problem attracting and keeping talent.

- The cost of living is higher in that particular city.

In any case, don't accept the offer without probing deeper.

Alternative 1: Without communicating surprise or concern, ask what factors were evaluated to arrive at the salary.

Alternative 2: Confirm the details of the benefits package (i.e., vacation, health insurance). Then, take a day or two and ask professionals outside the company what they would expect the salary to be.

Alternative 3: With or without mentioning the company's name, place an anonymous call to the human resources department of a competitor. Ask what they might expect the salary range for your position to be and why. To avoid being too specific, you might phrase this as a multiple choice question using salary ranges.

Unacceptable offers

For any negotiation to be successful, both parties must see the deal as fair. If you are unhappy with the stated salary, say so. Take the same dramatic pause that you would for an acceptable offer and say:

"In all honesty, the salary is below my expectations."

If you know you are worth more, stand firm. The company may have given you a low figure to see how you would react. If it becomes apparent that the company cannot meet your minimum salary requirements, use the opportunity to discuss alternatives:

"Perhaps we can balance our compensation objectives through performance-based bonuses, vacations, and other benefits."

By defending your value and understanding the company's financial constraints, you might discover that the position is less challenging or growth-oriented than you hoped. It's also possible that the company is just cheap. This is the time to find out.

Get it in writing

Once you reach an agreement, make sure all details are in writing. If the company doesn't take the initiative, you should. If possible, hand-deliver it. A written agreement won't be subject to the selective memory of people who may or may not be around in six months to honor it.

PART 3

The Product Life Cycle

The Growth Phase

If you board the wrong train, it is no use running along the corridor in the other direction.

—*DIETRICH BONHOEFFER*

CHAPTER 7

The Growth Phase

The View from the Bottom

You are the master of your personal development. Good bosses and coworkers may help you, but the ultimate responsibility is yours. The first few months in any job can be a wonderful opportunity to showcase your enthusiasm and your thinking. Never again will you have so much latitude. The initial freedom may ease some of the pressure, but it doesn't mean you can relax completely. Quite the contrary. In a healthy working environment, you will get patient assistance from your coworkers and mentors. Use this time to ask questions, demonstrate dedication, and earn respect.

As you progress, look for opportunities to recognize or assist your team. The best executives know that their success depends on the hard work of others. Mavericks don't typically excel in the corporate world.

Personality conflicts

No matter who you are, there will always be personalities that you find less than enjoyable. This can be particularly stressful in a working relationship because you won't have the option to ignore each other. For this reason, you owe it to yourself and your team to resolve conflicts quickly and directly. In doing so, remember two things:

- You can agree to disagree.

- It's always business, never personal.

The first point is valuable because it allows conflicting viewpoints to coexist. This way, no one has to be right. The second is valuable from a leadership standpoint because it reminds everyone to focus on common goals.

AND THE TROUBLE IS, IF YOU DON'T RISK ANYTHING, YOU RISK EVEN MORE.

—ERICA JONG

FORTUNE SIDES WITH HIM WHO DARES.

—VERGIL

Constructive criticism

When it becomes necessary to constructively criticize someone's performance, adopt two rules:

- Criticize the work, not the person.

- Praise in public, criticize in private.

Constructive criticism should take place behind closed doors to preserve the dignity of the people involved. Public embarrassment and ridicule are never good motivators.

Most people aren't malicious enough to intentionally aggravate others. When you disagree on matters of style, you can still maintain a healthy and productive working relationship. Communicate. Know what to expect. It will help everyone maintain their sanity.

Manage your reputation

Your reputation will always precede you. Make sure it's a good one. Here are a few suggestions to make this happen:

Be an advocate

Whenever possible, spotlight the efforts of others. Recognize people who have done exceptional work under difficult conditions. Thank them in a memo. Send a copy to their department supervisors. Describe what they did and why it made a difference. This will undoubtedly help during their next evaluation.

Make life easier

Every job has responsibilities that are time-consuming and frustrating. Eliminate a source of frustration and you will have a happier team. To put this into practice, I asked my secretary what one task she seriously disliked. (I was hoping it wasn't typing or answering phones.) To my surprise, she was most aggravated by requests to bring videotapes to the duplicating department. From that moment on, I made those trips myself. It took a few minutes out of my day, but the morale boost that it gave my secretary made it worth the effort.

From a psychological standpoint, the approach described above has powerful implications because it represents a tangible alternative to pay-raises. Money is not necessarily the best way to make a difficult job more satisfying (or less distasteful).

Manage expectations

Taking time to manage expectations and set reasonable limits is one of the best investments you can make. This is particularly important because certain professions tend to be a bit dysfunctional. Advertising, for example, attracts people who have a hard time saying "no." Even if you are already effective in setting limits, be careful. You could surround yourself with people who are not.

Over-servicing the client

For service-oriented companies, striving to meet client needs quickly and professionally is an admirable goal. Unfortunately, it can be problematic when the client is difficult, manipulative, or opportunistic. If you have any experience in the corporate world, you probably have examples of your own. If not, the following should suffice.

The events described below took place in the office of a large Leo Burnett client during a meeting between the product manager and a media sales rep. However, it could have happened anywhere. For this reason, it is not an indictment of dysfunctional agencies in general or Burnett in particular. Instead, it serves as a reminder of the following:

- Every industry is smaller than you think. Be discrete.

- In a corporation—particularly a service-oriented one—you are not the master of your schedule.

The meeting had just begun when the vice president of marketing interrupted to pass along a new advertising-related assignment. The product manager didn't stop to think just how well-connected media reps are. Otherwise, he would have been more discrete when the VP asked for an agency recommendation. (Like many multinational companies, this client maintained an arsenal of ad agencies.) Without hesitating, he delivered a truly backhanded compliment.

> "I'll give the project to Burnett. They'll have people working on it all night and we'll have an answer in the morning."

In the client's defense, expectations don't develop by accident. Companies train their clients well.

Ill-fated projects

In the corporate world, you don't have to be handcuffed by unreasonable expectations—but you might have to work hard to avoid it. Sometimes the best way to manage your time and reputation is first to manage your boss and client.

One of my most memorable real-life nightmares began in an early morning conference call. The client called to request a particularly complicated media project. From experience, I suspected that the required data would take at least three weeks to collect. The data analysis, strategic recommendation, and internal agency review would add at least another week. Although the realistic deadline would have been four weeks away, my boss promised the unachievable—a completed report within one week. When he told the client that I'd be project leader, I cringed.

Later that morning, the situation almost deteriorated. While my boss was at lunch, he received another call from the same client. I overheard our secretary taking a message as the client pushed the deadline up by four more days. My mind raced. Not entirely sure of my next step, I asked the secretary to transfer the call to my office. After the client quickly explained that his boss wanted the report by Monday, I took a deep breath and said:

> "I have to be honest with you. Ordinarily, the data would take three weeks to compile. The deadline we agreed to this morning was wildly optimistic and I'm doing everything possible to make sure we meet it. There is no way we will have anything by Monday."

To my surprise, I didn't encounter any resistance. Instead, he replied:

> "I didn't realize there was so much work involved. I'll let the people here know and we'll just review the report on Friday. Thanks for your help."

I knew my boss well enough to know that if he had taken the call, our new deadline would have been Monday and morale would have plummeted. As an advocate for the agency team, I didn't want to see that happen.

The Gift of Perspective

For my first few years in advertising, I couldn't believe anyone would pay me to have so much fun. Most days were like that. However, it was one not-so-fun day that my life changed for the better.

The day started like any other. I got to work not knowing exactly what to expect. Every day was different. That's why I liked it so much. Almost immediately, I received an urgent call from the client. The CEO wanted to see work-in-progress on a new advertising campaign. My mind raced.

Work-in-progress had taken on an entirely different meaning thanks to the client's complete inability to manage expectations. To them, work-in-progress meant a full-blown presentation complete with ads that looked ready for publication. Over 100 people would have to put in at least 24 hours of continuous work. Otherwise, there would be no ads and no presentation.

Within seconds of hanging up the phone, I contacted the key players whose support and teamwork I would need. We had quick meetings. We outlined our action plan. We called the art directors, copywriters, studios, photo labs, typesetters, and overnight couriers. Work orders were signed. Everyone knew what was expected. Everyone was doing their part. Nobody was happy about it.

Every meeting and phone call put me in touch with another distressed and angry soul. Before long, I too shared the community migraine created by the CEO's offhanded request. I left work frustrated and angry. The project would be completed on schedule, but the price—a huge blow to morale and $250,000 out of the budget—was extraordinary. It had been a terrible day and the day wasn't over yet.

That evening, my volunteer supervisor at Children's Memorial Medical Center asked me to see a 17-year-old patient. He didn't even look sick. He was energetic, enthusiastic, and happy. I was shocked when he told me he needed a new heart. For the first time all day, I was witness to a real problem. Despite the fact that he would die without a heart transplant, he had the most positive attitude I have ever seen.

I was truly ashamed of myself. None of the difficulty or frustration I had just faced at work compared to his life-threatening problems. Yet, he was confident and peaceful while I was preoccupied and depressed. Without knowing it, this courageous teenager taught me that no work-related issue deserves the attention, worry, power, or importance that I attached to the client's request. For this reason, he is one of several young patients who have been among my best teachers.

The wisdom I see in the patients at Children's continually renews my enthusiasm for life. At the same time, it reminds me that worrying is counterproductive—even when the issue is life and death. Sadly, most of what we worry about isn't even that serious.

FLOWERS GROW OUT OF DARK MOMENTS.

—CORITA KENT

Obstacles are opportunities

As exciting and challenging as corporate life can be, it's important to maintain perspective. Obstacles and challenges are part of any job. Some linger until you find the courage to face them. Others dissolve with deadlines only to be replaced by new issues and new deadlines. By gaining this perspective, I was better able to deal with the stress of time-sensitive outdoor advertising projects. Whenever the pressure would build, I'd smile and think:

> "Rob, people don't drive down the highway and say to themselves, 'That's a terrific billboard, but it should have been up last week.'"

Dealing with problems

Whether the problem is a deadline, your finances, or your health, it is nothing more than a circumstance. It has no intentions or feelings. It isn't subject to qualification (e.g., favorable or unfavorable). And it doesn't care what you think. It simply is. Don't use it as an excuse to trade your effectiveness for the deceptive comfort of self-pity.

IF SOMETHING COMES TO LIFE IN OTHERS BECAUSE OF YOU, THEN YOU HAVE MADE AN APPROACH TO IMMORTALITY.

—*NORMAN COUSINS*

Giving Back

Whatever your occupation, there will almost always be a nonprofit group that values your knowledge, skills, or resources. For example, you don't have to be a direct marketing or database expert to help a nonprofit organization create and manage a fund-raising mailing list. Likewise, artists and studios can collect outdated stock photo books, foamcore, and other expensive supplies to donate to a needy school. For the alert person, there are a wealth of opportunities to give back to the community. Your biggest challenge will not be what to do, but when to do it.

Listen to Your Dreams

As your career progresses, focus on what you have learned and how it relates to what you want to do. Know where you are, how you got there, and where you are going. Watch for opportunities.

In my case, it has always helped to believe that everything happens for a reason. Sometimes the reason is immediately apparent. Other times, it isn't. Either way, you don't have to accept the concept of a universal or divine plan to find value in every experience. It is as much an attitude as it is a belief.

NOT SIXTEEN PERCENT OF THE HUMAN RACE IS, OR EVER HAS BEEN, ENGAGED IN ANY OF THE KINDS OF ACTIVITY AT WHICH THEY EXCEL.

—MAIRET

Overleaf
Words & picture: Harry Wilson © 1996. From his forthcoming book of images and observations "I Wouldn't Have Missed It for Anything" (working title). Printed with permission.

For a planet bursting
with miracles.

For happiness
and sadness.

For what little
I accomplished
and even more that
I did not.

For warm hellos and
reluctant goodbyes.
So glad I came here.
I wouldn't have missed
it for anything.

Harry Wilson

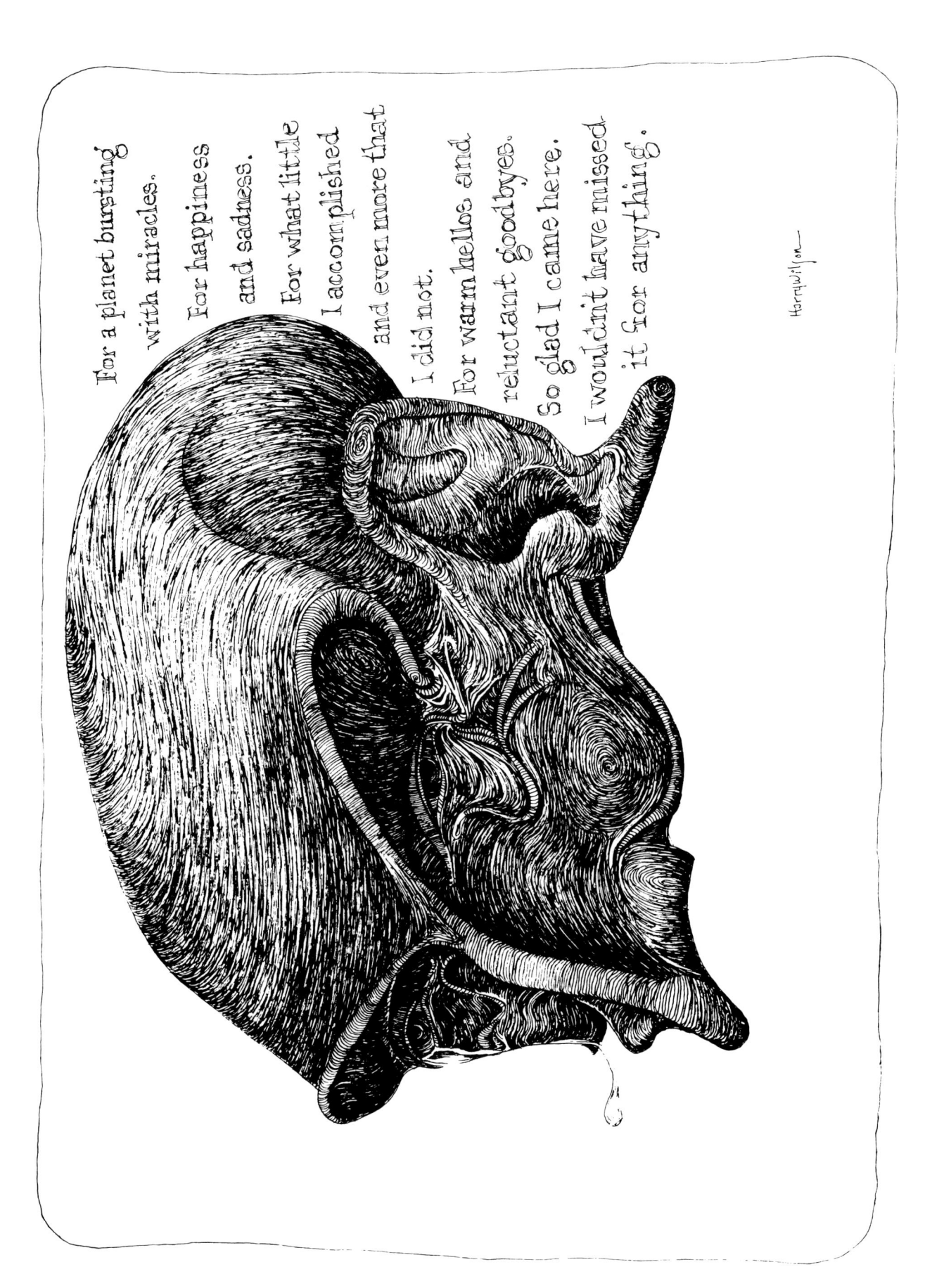

GREAT READING

Rather than provide the obligatory list of related reading material, I am including only those books that changed the way I approach life. Some are business books. Most are not. But all provide important insights into the meaning and value of life. Whether the goal is survival, self-improvement, or business success, these books are a source of power, positive thinking, motivation, and courage. Each, in its own way, has had a significant impact on the person I have become.

(Alphabetically by author)

"It's Easier Than You Think: The Buddhist Way to Happiness"
by Sylvia Boorstein
    If you don't have a background or interest in Eastern philosophy, this would be an easy book to pass over. Don't let that happen. Thanks to Sylvia Boorstein's matter-of-fact style, the chapters are clear, memorable, and concise. The insights are universal. And the path to happiness is accessible. To put it another way, enlightenment probably isn't what you think it is.
    HarperCollins Publishers, 10 East 53rd Street, New York, NY 10022

"Chicken Soup for the Soul: 101 Stories to Open the Heart and Rekindle the Spirit" written and compiled by Jack Canfield and Mark Victor Hansen
    A collection of anecdotes about the impact we can have on others—often without realizing it. These books deepened my appreciation for the people who have helped to shape my life. With each paragraph, my desire to have the same impact on others also grew. The stories are so thought-provoking (and short—one to two pages) that I often read one in the morning and another before I go to bed. The sequels are equally good.
    Health Communications, Inc. 3201 S.W. 15th Street, Deerfield Beach, FL 33442-8190

"How to Stop Worrying and Start Living" by Dale Carnegie
    A wonderful collection of techniques to eliminate the worry in your life. These true stories of overcoming stress, trauma, life- and career-threatening experiences are both memorable and inspirational. Although I read it almost six years ago, I remind myself of these techniques regularly.
    Simon & Schuster, 1230 Avenue of the Americas,
New York, NY 10020

"Man's Search For Meaning" by Viktor E. Frankl
    Frankl discusses his own struggle as a prisoner in the Nazi death camps during World War II. As a psychiatrist and survivor, he examines the role of motivation and the human desire to find meaning in existence—even when that existence defies understanding. I can only echo the thoughts of my college psychology professor who said, "Anyone who

even pretends to be educated should have read this book."
POCKET BOOKS, a division of Simon & Schuster, 1230 Avenue of the Americas, New York, NY 10020

"Creative Visualization" by Shakti Gawain
This is a step-by-step description of the meditations, exercises, and affirmations that are the basis for creative visualization. The process is often used for personal growth, health, and relaxation. A heart transplant patient that I know used these techniques to deal with pain.
New World Library, 58 Paul Drive, San Rafael, CA 94903

"Death Be Not Proud: A Memoir" by John Gunther
A true story about the author's son, Johnny Gunther, who died at age 17 of a brain tumor. Courage, faith, patience, perspective, and intelligence are words that only begin to capture the spirit of this book.
Harper & Row, Publishers, Inc., 10 East 53rd Street, New York, NY 10022

"What Was Good About Today" by Carol Kruckeberg
A truly moving story about the author's 8-year-old daughter Sara. From the initial diagnosis of leukemia to her untimely death, Sara's spunk and positive energy rarely wavered. Despite her pain and prognosis, Sara and her family finished every day by answering the title's question: "What was good about today?" Deeply moving, yet hopeful.
Madrona Publishers, 3202 Fuhrman East, Seattle, WA 98102

"The Way of the Peaceful Warrior" by Dan Millman
In this engaging story of self-discovery, Dan befriends a gas station attendant named Socrates who, through a series of late-night conversations, becomes his mentor. With wit, wisdom, compassion, and a collection of bizarre experiences, Socrates helps Dan replace his inner confusion and cynicism with peace and understanding. This book is to emotional and personal development what *"The Celestine Prophecy"* is to the forces at work in the universe.
H.J. Kramer, Inc., P.O. Box 1082, Tiburon, CA 94920

"The World Up Close: A Cyclist's Adventures on Five Continents" by Kameel Nasr
This is the story of the author's 40,000-mile bicycle trek across the globe. Even more memorable than Nasr's descriptions of the countries are his insights about the people. For all of their cultural barriers, Nasr and the people he encountered found ways to communicate and enjoy each other's differences without relying on language, laws, or government. This book is as much about human relations as it is about adventure. After traveling through North and South America, India, Thailand, Japan, Africa—70 countries in all—Nasr reached this conclusion:

> "The biggest obstacle facing travelers is not dishonest people or wild animals or bad roads; it is not disease or food or bad water or diverse languages. Problems make travel an adven-

ture which can, depending on a mixture of the traveler's ability and attitude and luck, enrich the traveler's life. The biggest obstacle to travelers is government."

Mills & Sanderson, Box 665, Bedford, MA 01730

"Ogilvy On Advertising" by David Ogilvy

This is the book that got me excited about advertising. Ogilvy's colorful style and insight made me wish that I could have lived through his years at Ogilvy & Mather.

Random House, Inc., 201 E. 50th Street, 22nd Floor, New York, NY 10022

"The Celestine Prophecy" by James Redfield

An adventure of discovery and understanding that revolves around the search for a series of nine manuscripts. Each describes an insight essential to understanding the nature of life itself and our place on this planet. If nothing else, you will pay more attention to coincidences.

I know so many people with strong and opposite feelings about this book that I must also include a word of caution. This is not a literary masterpiece. If you are a critical reader, don't let your feelings about the writing or story-line camouflage the value of this work.

Warner Books, Inc., 1271 Avenue of the Americas, New York, NY 10020

"Entrepreneurs Are Made, Not Born: Secrets from 200 Successful Entrepreneurs" by Lloyd E. Shefsky

A factual and inspirational reference for anyone who has ever considered starting their own business. This book opens the mind to different ways of thinking. By the time I read the last page, I had three solid, original ideas for starting my own company.

McGraw-Hill, Inc., 1221 Avenue of the Americas, New York, NY 10020

"A Whack on the Side of the Head: How You Can Be More Creative" by Roger von Oech

A fun and involving book that examines ways to stimulate your creative potential. Loaded with great questions, puzzles, stories, and mental challenges.

Warner Books, Inc., 1271 Avenue of the Americas, New York, NY 10020

GLOSSARY

A

Account management - *(advertising/marketing)* Often described as the "hub of the wheel," this department represents the advertising agency to the client and the client to the agency. Responsibilities include coordinating the efforts of the agency teams (e.g., creative, research, media, production, legal), overseeing the budget, daily contact with client to identify and address needs, finding opportunities to move the client's business ahead, etc. This department typically includes assistant account executives (entry-level), account executives, account supervisors, and account directors.

Attribute - *product:* a quality, feature, or characteristic that may give rise to a product BENEFIT.

B

Benefit - 1. *product:* any aspect of a product that somehow improves the life of the person using it (e.g., saves time, tastes better) 2. non-monetary form of compensation (e.g., insurance, health club membership).

C

Copy - The words used in an ad.

Cover letter - a short (one-page), introductory communication sent to potential employers or networking contacts along with a RÉSUMÉ. The letter addresses the following issues: who you are, why you are writing, what you have to offer, and how it addresses the company's needs.

Creative - *(advertising)* 1. a person who works in the creative department (i.e., art director, copywriter). 2. the advertising itself (e.g., television commercial, print ad, radio spot, storyboard, concept).

D

Distance test - a method of viewing the résumé at a distance of five to seven feet to objectively assess its most prominent selling messages. A well-planned, skill-focused résumé can begin to answer important questions about a candidate's potential even at a distance. An unfocused résumé, viewed at the same distance, will not distinguish one candidate from another.

H

Headhunter - a professional who matches executives with companies. Headhunters often specialize in particular industries (e.g., advertising) and represent both companies and individuals. Once a match is made, the hiring company typically pays the headhunter a commission based on a predetermined percentage of the candidate's first year salary.

I

Inherent drama - the compelling quality or uniqueness of a product or service. That property which becomes the basis for meaningful advertising. *Also:* UNIQUE SELLING PROPOSITION.

Informational interview - a meeting in which the candidate makes it clear that the objective is not to ask for a job but to gather information, insight, and guidance.

Interview - a conversation between a potential employer and a job candidate during which both parties evaluate mutual fit. The potential employer wants answers to the following questions:

- Is this person right for the job?

- Does he or she have the necessary skills/potential?

- Do I want this person on my team?

Likewise, the candidate attempts answers to the following questions:

- Is this position the best use of my talents and interests?

- Does the company provide an environment in which I can grow both personally and professionally?

- Will I be happy working with these people?

See also: INFORMATIONAL INTERVIEW; MOCK INTERVIEW; STRESS INTERVIEW.

M

Marketing plan - a document that describes a particular product or service and the strategies and tactics that will be employed to sell or promote it. This plan includes a review of the current business environment including potential customers, competitors, and geographic opportunities.

Mock interview - a practice interview with a career counselor or other person willing to provide objective feedback and constructive criticism. Videotaped mock interviews give the candidate an opportunity to observe his or her performance while paying particular attention to behavior, body language, and other unconscious or unintended communication.

N

Negotiation - the process through which two parties seek to balance their individual objectives. For a negotiation to be successful, both parties must feel that they secured a fair deal.

O

Objective - a stated goal or purpose. *Job hunting:* a brief description of the information or position being sought. (The objective is more effective in the first paragraph of a cover letter than on a résumé).

P

Positioning - *product:* what the product is, who it is for, and why it is better than competitive products.

Product Life Cycle - a marketing concept that categorizes consumer goods according to market acceptance/competitive position (sales/market share) and financial return for the company (profitability). According to this theory, a product would move through four phases:

Phase I: Introduction
Slow rise in sales often accompanied by heavy marketing spending to stimulate awareness/trial/sales.

Phase II: Growth
Sales increase rapidly. Company may face a trade-off between high sales (market share) and profit. At this point, the brand management team must decide whether the profit per dollar of incremental sales justifies the additional marketing expense (e.g., advertising, promotion, distribution).

Phase III: Maturity
Sales growth slows, stabilizes and may begin to decline.

Phase IV: Decline - Technological advances, consumer taste, pricing pressure, competitive activity, or other marketing factors may reduce sales/profits.

(continued on next page)

Product Life Cycle *(continued)*

For marketers who accept the concept of the Product Life Cycle, categorizing a particular product is more than an academic exercise. The point where a product is determined to fall on the curve can have a material impact on marketing and promotional support.

The author exercised "creative license" with regard to the product life cycle/ growth phase referred to in Part III of this book. The sharp, vertical ascent of the learning curve better describes the personal marketing opportunities that arise during the first few months of employment. However, *Climbing Your Way to the Bottom* is based on the similarities between selling yourself and selling a product. Given that constraint, the rapid growth phase is that section of the product life cycle curve that most closely parallels the first stage of the learning curve. If you find this confusing, don't worry. This discussion is included only as clarification for truly rigorous readers who have a low tolerance for inconsistency.

R

Résumé - a one-page, concept-intensive document used to distinguish one faceless candidate from another. After taking the time to understand the needs of the potential employer, the résumé writer incorporates relevant skills and experiences. In simple English, the résumé is:

"Your life on one page as it relates to the job of your dreams."

S

Stress interview - an interview in which the potential employer creates an uncomfortable situation to evaluate the candidate's ability to handle it. Common techniques include rapid-fire questions, a hostile/confrontational attitude (or constant devil's advocate)—even absolute silence.

T

Target - the intended recipient(s) of a communication.

U

Unique Selling Proposition (USP) - the compelling quality or uniqueness of a product or service. That property which becomes the basis for meaningful advertising. *Also:* INHERENT DRAMA.

INDEX

A

attribute (product) 83-84, 94, 100
   example 84, 98

B

Barenboim, Daniel 42
benefit (product) 83-84, 95, 98
   example 84, 98
Beethoven, Ludwig van 106
Bolles, Richard Nelson *xxxi*
Bradley Communications 59
Burnett, Leo 85, 86, 113
   agency recruiting 72, 85, 106

C

Carnegie, Dale 113
category analysis 15-17
Chicago Symphony Orchestra 42
Children's Memorial Medical Center (Chicago) 129
cover letters *xxxiii*, 5, 21-22, 24-31, 37, 41, 44, 47-48, 50, 53, 60, 89
   content 26-27
   objective 26
   sample 28-29, 48, 50
criticism (constructive) 126

D

Do What You Love and the Money Will Follow. See Sinetar, Marsha
Dow, Jerry 43

F

Floyd, Jim 58-59

G

gifts 61
GMAT (Graduate Management Admissios Test) 5
Grande Sonata Pathétique. See Beethoven.

H

help wanted ads 56
   anonymous 56, 57
hobbies 11, 43, 49, 51, 106

I

improvisation (as a way to control nervousness) 113-114
interview questions 77, 94
   accomplishment 94
   adjective list (self-assessment) 77, 86-88
   continuum (self-assessment) 99-100
   creative assessment 77
   inappropriate 101-102
interviews *xxxiii*, 75-83, 94
   concept of 21
   defined 73
   dressing for 72
   informational 26, 52-55, 68-71
   mock 67, 108
   multiple 60
   positive traits 78
   preparation 47, 55
   stress 93-94
   videotaped 67

J

job ads. *See help wanted.*
job offers. *See negotiation.*

K

Kotler, Philip 25

L

LSAT (Law School Admissions Test) 5

M

MBA (Master's in Business Administration) 8, 19, 79, 80
Moody Blues 42

N

negotiation 115-120
networking 54, 55

O

offers. *See negotiation.*
Ogilvy on Advertising
   David Ogilvy 17

P

Players' Workshop (Chicago) 113
product attribute. *See attribute.*
product benefit. *See benefit.*

R

Radio/TV Interview Reports. See Bradley Communications
résumé 30-52
   samples 34-37, 49, 51

S

salary 115
   history 117
   negotiation 115-120
SAT (Scholastic Aptitude Test) 5
Second City 113
self-analysis 8-12
Sinetar, Marsha 79
Solti, Sir Georg 42
Star Wars 85

T

thank you notes 60

W

What Color is Your Parachute? See Bolles, Richard Nelson.
WUSN-FM 60

To order additional books, please visit your local bookstore. Or, to order books directly from the publisher, send $22.95 for soft cover ($29.95 for hard cover) plus $4.50 postage and handling. Illinois residents please add 8 3/4% sales tax. Allow 30 days for delivery. For faster delivery options and rates, please call 1-800-MY-CLIMB.

>Pure Play Publishing
>2501 N. Lincoln Ave.
># 167 B
>Chicago, IL 60614
>312-409-9448
>http://www.pureplay.com/pureplay
>
>VISA/MasterCard orders call:
>**1-800-MY-CLIMB**
>(1-800-692-5462)

Prices subject to change without notice. Quantity discounts available.

NEWSLETTER ALERT

As an on-going service to readers, Rob Sullivan is developing a newsletter that addresses job hunting issues and questions. For a free sample and subscription information, send your name and address to:

>Rob Sullivan
>c/o PurePlay publishing
>2501 N. Lincoln Ave. #167
>Chicago, IL 60614
>e- mail: rsullivn@pureplay.com